A BEAUTIFUL MINE

WOMEN PROSPECTORS OF THE OLD WEST

Chris Enss

TWODOT®

GUILFORD, CONNECTICUT
HELENA, MONTANA
AN IMPRINT OF THE GLOBE PEQUOT PRESS

To buy books in quantity for corporate use
or incentives, call **(800) 962–0973**
or e-mail **premiums@GlobePequot.com.**

A · TWODOT® · BOOK

Copyright © 2008 by Chris Enss

TwoDot is a registered trademark of The Globe Pequot Press.

Text design by Lisa Reneson

Library of Congress Cataloging-in-Publication Data is available.

ISBN 978-0-7627-4372-8

Printed in the United States of America

10 9 8 7 6 5 4 3 2 1

For Patti Ferree, who, like Nellie Cashman,
is a smart businesswoman and shows compassion
to everyone, including prisoners wrongly accused.

CONTENTS

ACKNOWLEDGMENTS

I am indebted to the many librarians who help to make history books like these possible. Every biographer of a person of an earlier era owes much to the adequacy of libraries and the skill of the librarians. I am particularly grateful to Joyce M. Cox, the head of reference services at the Nevada State Library and Archives in Carson City. She was gracious, kind, and infinitely patient. She made available files, old letters, scrapbooks, and newspaper articles about many of the women miners who lived and worked in Nevada.

Invaluable in the research efforts were historians Ed Tyson, with the Searls Historical Library in Nevada City, California, and Kathleen Correia at the California State Library History Room. The staff of archivists at the Denver Public Library, the Arizona Historical Society, the Vancouver Public Library, and the Glenbow Museum in Calgary, Alberta, Canada were also generous with their time and assistance.

Special acknowledgments are due to my editor, Erin Turner, for her thoughtful counsel on this and other books I have been blessed to pen, and to my publisher Globe Pequot Press for the opportunities they have given me.

INTRODUCTION

"This morning the gold fever raged so high that I went again to dig with the rest but got very little gold. Came home tired tonight. Still in good spirits."
—Prospector Lucena Parsons, August 1851

A parade of prospectors trudged up and down the dusty foot-paths through a rustic mining camp at the base of California's Sierra Mountain Range near Gold Canyon. The hills around the bustling burg were clothed in Douglas fir trees, and a line of rocky bluffs peered down on the busy Argonauts hurrying about. Some carried pans and picks and shovels; others shook rockers back and forth in a nearby stream. One of the miners diligently sifted through gravel and deposited a handful of gold nuggets into a leather pouch tied tightly to a rope belt around the waist. Perspiration beaded across the prospector's forehead; the ambitious worker removed a floppy brimmed hat to dab the sweat away, revealing a mass of black hair piled into a bun. The hard-working woman brushed the dust off her calico shirt, tucked her trousers into her boot socks, and returned to her job.

The presence of a woman miner among a sea of male prospec-tors was rare but hardly a distraction for those in a fever for gold or silver. As the woman passed by the other miners on the way to her

Three women pose in front of tents somewhere between their claims on Spruce Creek in the Atlin mining district in Alaska, circa 1899.

tent, the majority of men continued on with their work, offering her little more than a glance. The few who took a moment to contemplate a female in their midst tipped their hats and nodded to her. She smiled politely back at them, focused more on the profitable results of the day's labor than anything else.

It is estimated that less than five thousand women were a part of the horde that flooded California in the gold rush of 1849. The sin-filled, hell-raising mining camps welcomed with open arms the women who sold their bodies by the hour, respected the wives and daughters who cared for their spouses and fathers, and merely toler-ated ladies who worked outside the home in occupations other than prostitution and cooking. The mine field was the least likely place one would think to find a woman in the mid-1800s, but adventurous females possessing the same passion for riches as their male coun-terparts dared to subject themselves to countless hardships and per-sonal recriminations to locate their own strike.

Not only was mining an unconventional role for women, it was also a hazardous, back-breaking job that involved wading in and out of cold streams and riverbeds picking through sand and gravel, and hoisting mounds of earth to the surface in bucket and wheel excavations. Most women miners were willing to tolerate any hardship to find a fortune and even developed a fondness for the work, while others questioned their decision to venture into the career at all. In 1851, would-be miner Louise Clappe admitted her misgivings about the profession in her journal. "I am sorry I learned the trade," she wrote, "for I wet my feet, tore my dress, spoilt a pair of new gloves, nearly froze my fingers, got an awful headache, took cold and lost a valuable breastpin, in this my labor of love."

Lady prospectors like Nellie Cashman and Ellen Nay couldn't envision life without mining. They trekked over rugged terrain, enduring below-freezing temperatures in the Alaskan wilderness and scorching heat in California's Death Valley in order to reach outcroppings rumored to hold a treasure of yellow nuggets. Baby Doe Tabor of Colorado inherited her gold mine but sank every dime she had into the diggings, oftentimes sacrificing food and heat in the process.

Ethel Berry lived in a small cabin with dirt floors and flour sack curtains and panned for gold by lamplight before making a

PHOTO CREDIT: YUKON ARCHIVES, ANTON VOGEE FONDS, #9056

Although clad in silk skirts, taffeta hats, and velvet jackets, these lady miners along the Bonanza Creek in the Yukon Territory weren't opposed to dressing in trousers and flannel shirts and digging alongside their male counterparts to find a fortune of their own.

wealthy discovery. Miner and author Dame Shirley witnessed the struggle and sometimes the death of ambitious miners and their families, and she translated a prospector's endeavors into a series of detailed and moving magazine articles that were read by Argonauts from Monterey to Death Valley.

Convinced women could not withstand the difficulties associated with mining, a number of male prospectors agreed to tolerate their company until they gave up and went home. "I've seen one or two females digging and panning, but it won't amount to much," forty-niner Caleb MacDonald wrote in his journal in early 1850. "They'll head back to civilization when winter sets in."

PHOTO CREDIT: YUKON ARCHIVES, ADAMS & LARKIN FONDS, #61

Lady miners hoping to discover gold in the Klondike had to travel the thirty-three-mile-long Chilkoot Trail that wound through the Coast Mountains.

Nevada prospector Josie Pearl was one of the first lady miners to prove that women had staying power. "Gold is devilish stuff and mining is a beautiful way of life. It gets into your blood and you can't leave it alone, and Lordy! I should know if anyone does! Why, I've been worth $100,000 one day and the next day I've had nothing and had to go to work for $30 a month in some mining camp. You know, I can do practically anything I make up my mind to do."

Years of hard working and privation paid off for lady miners like Dr. Frances Williams of Nevada. Her claims yielded more than $2 million in gold ore. Downieville, California, resident Gertrude Peckwith, however, never made a substantial find. Luck didn't care if the digger was a man or a woman—it favored anyone who worked as hard as fourteen hours a day, seven days a week.

From the moment the first cry of "Gold!" echoed over the plains, women prospectors followed the news west. From Fairbanks, Alaska, to Cripple Creek, Colorado, lady miners labored long and hard to develop digs, pulling from the earth mineral deposits ranging from silver to coal. In the process, lady miners dug out for themselves a unique place in history.

BABY DOE TABOR:
QUEEN OF THE MATCHLESS MINE

"The bride is a veritable beauty—blonde, with face and form alike almost ideal in their lovely proportions."

—*Washington Post,* March 3, 1883

A shabby-looking prospector emerged from the dark, weathered entrance of the Matchless Mine in Leadville, Colorado, and straightened his stooped shoulders. He dropped his pickax beside a rusty ore cart and rolled and lit a cigarette. His weary face was set in a scowl as he surveyed the mountains rising precipitately around the well-worked diggings. The smoke from the chimney of a nearby shack rose into the air and drifted towards him. As he watched the smoke swirl and evaporate into a vibrant blue sky, an elderly woman charged out of the building into the cold.

Seventy-five-year-old Baby Doe Tabor was dressed in layers of torn, threadbare garments that dragged along the ground. Her woolen hat sat just above her azure eyes, and she wore a ragged leather boot on one foot and a cluster of rags, bound by a strip of material, on the other. As she made her way toward the miner a slight smile stretched across her hollowed cheeks. "What did you find?" she asked him hopefully. The man shook his head. A flash of

1

irritation erupted in her eyes but quickly dissipated as she scanned the colorful horizon.

Baby Doe's late husband was Horace Tabor, the Silver King. He made and lost a fortune in mining. At one time the country around her was swarming with workers who pulled millions out of the diggings where she lived. It had been more than thirty years since the mine had yielded anything but dust and rock. Baby Doe stayed on the property because of a deathbed promise she made to Horace. "Never let the Matchless go if I die, Baby. It will make millions again when silver comes back."

She had implicit faith in her husband's judgment and in the Matchless, but she was alone in her belief. The only men who would agree to venture into the mine in 1929 were drifters or one-time hopeful prospectors. Baby Doe persuaded them to dig in exchange for shares in the potential find.

The disheveled miner took a look around, gathered up his few belongings, and tramped through the snow out of camp. Baby Doe's eyes followed the prospector until he disappeared into a grove of pine trees. "Hang on to the Matchless," she whispered to herself. "Horace told me it would make millions again."

The poverty and degradation that Baby Doe experienced in her last few years on earth were in direct contrast to the time she spent as the wife of a mining mogul. Born Elizabeth Bonduel McCourt in 1854 to a family of moderate means in Oshkosh, Wisconsin, she maneuvered her way around Colorado's high society until she met a man who would liberate her from her lackluster background. Her parents were Irish immigrants from County Armagh who had escaped the turmoil in their own country and initially settled in Utica, New York. They had fourteen children, many of whom died in infancy.

Elizabeth's angelic face, golden locks, and striking blue eyes set her apart from the other children. Elizabeth's father, a tailor and the owner of a clothing store, doted on her. Oftentimes he brought the girl to work with him and customers raved about her beauty. On more than one occasion businessmen would ask if her father wasn't afraid "someone would steal her away." Baby Doe thrived on the attention of the male clientele and learned at a young age how to manipulate them into giving her whatever she asked for.

Elizabeth's stunning looks continued to improve as she got older. At fifteen she was 5'2" with long, blonde hair, a robust figure, and sun-kissed porcelain skin. Men of all ages hovered around her like frantic bees at a hive. She received several marriage proposals but refused the sincere suitors in favor of pursuing a career on the stage. She was also determined to wed a man of great wealth.

The bold teenager dismissed the admonitions of her brothers and sisters to behave sensibly, abandon the notion of acting, settle down. Although there were a few respected actresses in the late 1870s, for the most part female thespians were considered to be just a slight step above prostitutes. Elizabeth didn't care what "polite society" thought of her. She was driven by an independent spirit her father had nurtured and her dreams of fame and money.

In December 1876, Elizabeth participated in a skating contest hosted by the Congregational Church. Boldly sporting a skirt that revealed her calves, she gracefully twirled through a routine, exciting the male onlookers and enraging female audience members. At the end of the competition, Elizabeth had captured a first place ribbon and the heart of handsome socialite, Harvey Doe.

Elizabeth was attracted to Harvey for a variety of reasons, not the least of which was the fact that he was heir to a mining dynasty. William Harvey Doe Sr. owned a substantial number of mining

Elizabeth Bonduel McCourt, better known as Baby Doe, poses for the camera in her finest garments. Note that the fur coat and hat are dusted with fake snow.

claims in Colorado. Doe also owned a lumber business in Oshkosh and had returned with his son to check on his investment at the same time the skating event was being held. Harvey was quite smitten with Elizabeth, and her parents found the young man charming and personable. Mrs. Doe, however, objected to her son spending time with a girl she considered to be a "daring exhibitionist." Harvey disregarded his mother's complaints about Elizabeth's parents' financial standing and her view of the girl as a "social climber." He proclaimed his love for Elizabeth and proposed marriage.

Elizabeth's recollection of Harvey's proposal was that it was the first such invitation that had "moved her deeply." According to what she shared with a friend in the 1930s, Harvey was different from the other men in town who sought her affections. "He would come over to play the piano for all my family in the evening, seeming to love us all. He would join in the general fun without trying to monopolize me, like other men."

On June 27, 1877, Harvey and Elizabeth were married at her parents' home. Immediately after the ceremony the couple boarded a train bound for Denver, Colorado. Harvey Doe Sr. planned for his son to take over the mining property in nearby Central City.

Once the newlyweds had finished honeymooning they would embark on a life in the gold fields of Pikes Peak. Elizabeth's father-in-law made arrangements for her and her new husband to reside at a posh hotel called the Teller House. The inn was elegant and decorated with the finest European furniture and rugs.

Elizabeth was enthusiastic about her new home, and the luxurious living conditions were precisely what she had envisioned for herself. She was also enchanted with the activity at the Fourth of July Mine where Harvey worked. The sights and sounds of the miners descending into the diggings and reappearing with chunks of earth that might be gold stirred her desire for outrageous wealth.

At the time Baby believed the opportunity to amass a fortune could only be realized through Harvey's efforts. Doe Sr. wanted his son to earn his profits and reputation the same way he had: by working in every area of the mining development, from collecting ore to operating the stamp mill. Harvey, however, wasn't interested in manual labor and preferred anyone else to do the work. Elizabeth was far too ambitious to leave the future of her financial status to a lazy husband and quickly took command of the property and limited income. After moving their belongings out of the expensive hotel where they had been living and into a small cottage, she organized a crew of Cornish miners to work at the Fourth of July Mine.

Some of the prominent town leaders with whom Elizabeth was acquainted advised her to have a shaft dug into the mine before winter fully set in. Joseph Thatcher, president of the First National Bank, and Bill Bush, owner of the Teller House, were two men whose opinion she respected the most. They urged her to do the digging herself if necessary.

Motivated by his wife's drive, Harvey finally bent to her will and joined in the work. The first shaft the pair sank proved to be unsuccessful; there was no high-grade ore in that section of the mine. Elizabeth was not going to give up. She convinced her husband and their employees to drive a second shaft. Dressed in one of Harvey's old shirts, a pair of dungarees, and a cap, Elizabeth toiled alongside the men.

In early October 1878, the editor of a mining newspaper in Central City was traveling through the busy area when he noticed the petite young woman lifting timbers and hauling tailings to a nearby pile. An article in the next edition of the paper included news about the woman prospector:

> I next reached the Fourth of July lode, a mine which has not been worked for several years, but started up some months ago under the personal supervision of the owner, Mr. W. H. Doe and his wife. The young lady manages one half of the property while her liege lord manages the other. I found both of their separate shafts managing a number of workmen, Mr. Doe at his which is seventy feet, and his wife, who is full of ambition, in her new enterprise, at hers which is sunk sixty feet. This is the first instance where a lady, and such she is, has managed a mining property. The mine is doing very well and produces some rich ore.

Briefly it seemed that Elizabeth and Harvey were striving together for a common goal. The pair diligently worked their claim, leaving the mine only to collect supplies in town. Historians speculate that it was during one of those trips when Elizabeth acquired the name by which she would be more commonly known. Rough, outspoken miners congregated outside saloons and mercantiles, talking with one another and swapping stories about their prospecting adventures. As Elizabeth passed by the men on her way to purchase food and various odds and ends, one man called out, "There goes a beautiful baby." The handle suited her diminutive frame and delicate features and from that time on she was referred to by most as "Baby Doe."

Despite the Does' valiant efforts, the Fourth of July Mine never yielded the gold necessary to fund continued diggings. Harvey borrowed money to keep the operation going, but it was ultimately shut down. He went to work for another miner and abandoned his dream of striking it rich. Baby Doe held onto her aspiration of becoming a "woman of great means." She was determined to realize that dream with or without Harvey.

Baby voiced her disappointment to Harvey about his lack of business sense and drive, and he drank a lot as a way to cope with her criticism. They spent a great deal of time apart, he at the saloons and she at a fabric and clothing store called Sandelowsky-Pelton. Baby's father-in-law returned to the area to try to help the pair get beyond their financial difficulties. He sold the Fourth of July Mine and settled their outstanding debts, but it couldn't save Baby and Harvey's relationship. By the summer of 1878, the two were leading virtually separate lives.

Baby spent a great deal of time with Jake Sandelowsky, the distinguished and handsome co-owner of the store she frequented. Her actions scandalized the town and infuriated Harvey. She defended Jake to her husband, making mention of the financial support the businessman had given her. She wasn't shy about reminding Harvey that what she wanted most in life was financial independence. Desperate to save his marriage, Harvey worked extra shifts to provide his wife with a quality of life that would make her happy. Jake seized the time during his absence to shower Baby with attention. He was her frequent escort to a local theater and saloon called the Shoo-Fly. Jake tried to persuade her to leave Harvey and marry him, but he didn't possess the riches Baby hoped to make her own. She decided to remain married to Harvey until a truly better offer came along.

News that gold had been played out in Central City rapidly filtered through the Shoo-Fly clientele in November 1878. Silver veins had been located around the area, however, generating a surge of eager mine investors. Among the men with the capital to sink numerous shafts and extract the mineral was Horace Tabor. He had become rich with similar mines in Leadville and hoped to duplicate his success in Central City. Baby knew of Horace and had caught sight of the entrepreneur at the Shoo-Fly but had not been formerly introduced. Before the possibility of a meeting was realized, Baby learned she was pregnant.

For several months Harvey was nowhere to be found and could not be told that he had a child on the way. There was some speculation that he had snuck away to a nearby mining camp to avoid the humiliation of his wife's questionable behavior with another man. Harvey Doe Sr. located his son and brought him home to Baby.

On July 13, 1879, Baby gave birth to a boy. The child was still-born and both parents were crushed. Harvey was further devastated by the rumors circulating that the child might not have been his. Baby was discouraged by Harvey's inability to pay any of the medical bills or make arrangements for the infant's burial. Jake Sandelowsky came to Baby's rescue and took care of matters. The Does divorced in early 1880 and Baby left Central City for Leadville with Jake.

Jake and Baby lived at separate hotels. Although he had planned for their relationship to blossom, Baby had other ideas for her life. Everywhere she went in Leadville she heard stories about Horace Tabor. Tales of his wealth and how he achieved it, his benevolence to average citizens, his term as first mayor and postmaster of the city, his time as governor of Colorado, and his reputation as owner operator of the Leadville Bank excited the industrious beauty from Wisconsin. She set her sights on meeting and befriending Horace. Jake would be a means to an end.

"He must be close to fifty," a friendly Leadville resident shared with Baby when she asked to know more about Horace. "They say he's worth $8 million and likes to play poker in the saloons around town after the theater lets out. He was one of the early prospectors out here—came in an ox-wagon across the plains in '59. An awful easygoing sort of fellow."

Baby listened intently to every detail of Tabor's life that the talkative local man shared. She learned that the mine owner panned out his first millions in the gold stampede on Colorado's Gregory Gulch, that he grubstaked two miners who discovered a wealth of silver at the Little Pittsburgh Mine, and that he used the money from his investments to buy a claim called the Matchless Mine. She ignored the details about his longstanding marriage to a refined woman who possessed a considerable strength of character, and focused instead on the name of the restaurant Horace frequented. It was not a coincidence that she ended up at the same establishment the "Silver King" visited during intermission at the Opera House.

"He was over six feet tall with large, regular features and a drooping mustache," Baby recounted years later to a young woman who spent time with her at her famous mine. "Dark in coloring, at this time his hair had begun to recede a bit on his forehead and was turning gray at the temples. Always very well dressed, his personality seemed to fill any room he stepped into."

Horace noticed Baby almost from the moment he entered the eatery. They exchanged polite glances and eventually one of his business associates invited Baby to join them at their table. Horace ordered champagne and regaled the captivated Baby with tales of his ventures west. "It was the merriest night of my life," Baby later confessed. By the end of the evening she was convinced she was in love with Horace and he was equally as infatuated with her. He promised to support Baby monetarily and as his first order of business, he wrote out a check for $5,000 to help ease Jake Sandelowsky's soon-to-be broken heart. Funds were also provided for Baby to purchase herself a new wardrobe.

Within twenty-four hours of meeting the businessman and appointed Governor, Baby had become Horace Tabor's mistress. They tried to keep their relationship a secret. Tabor would sneak away from various civic events to spend time with Baby at her hotel room, and when she appeared in public with him, she hid her face under large hats and long veils.

When Horace moved his mining offices from Leadville to Denver, Baby followed him. Friends and business associates aware of the scandalous romance tried to persuade him to end the affair for his family's sake and for the sake of his political future. Horace refused. The longer their relationship lasted, the bolder their behavior became. They traveled back and forth to Leadville together in private railcars and openly attended parties at various stops along the way.

Horace had a special box for Baby at the Opera House he had built. According to Baby Doe, at the opening of the Tabor Theatre on September 5, 1881, she and Horace eyed one another fondly during the performance. Horace's wife Augusta was eventually made aware of the affair but refused to divorce her husband; she considered divorce a social and moral disgrace. After close to two years of pleading and negotiating with Augusta, Horace brought his marital woes to a judge in Durango who granted the millionaire a divorce.

On September 30, 1882, Baby Doe and Horace rendezvoused in St. Louis, Missouri, where they were secretly married by a justice of the peace. Although Baby was grateful that Horace had taken her to the altar, his failure to divorce Augusta left her disappointed. "I tried to pretend I was as happy as he," she recounted to a friend. "But to me, a marriage was only binding when it had been sanctioned by the church and performed by a priest."

In January 1883, a few weeks prior to the senatorial election in which Horace Tabor was a candidate, Augusta agreed to a legal divorce. The specifics of the settlement and circumstances leading up to Augusta's decision were front-page headlines. The highly publicized affair detracted from the real issues of the election and ultimately cost Horace a seat in the senate. He was, however, asked to stand in for the winning candidate for a month until the newly elected official could take over his duties. It was with a heavy heart that Horace accepted the responsibility. Although he was disappointed in the vote, he found solace in the fact that he would soon be married in a church in Washington, D.C.

On March 1, 1883, Baby Doe was escorted down the aisle of the St. Matthew's Catholic Church, wearing a $7,500 wedding dress and beaming at the attendees, who included President Chester A. Arthur and the Secretary of the Interior, Henry Teller. The majority of the wives of the political figures who were guests at Horace and Baby's wedding refused to be a part of the ceremony in any way. They spoke out against what they called an "unholy union" and considered it poor taste that the "shameless mistress" sent invitations at all.

Elated by the fact that they were now legally and finally married, and optimistic that Horace's political career would be rejuvenated, the newlyweds returned to Denver. They moved into the Windsor Hotel and entertained celebrities and Civil War heroes in their suites. They traveled about the state making stops in various mining camps in what the two secretly discussed as a precursor to a much larger tour coming their way once Horace became president of the United States. "First lady of Colorado. Hell!" Horace told his wife. "You'll be first lady of the land."

In between making their elaborate plans for the future, the Tabors purchased the first of two grand brick homes. The house featured fine furnishings, ornate verandahs, driveways to the stables, and hundreds of live peacocks. An army of servants attended to the couple's every need. On July 13, 1884, Horace and Baby Doe brought their first child into the luxurious setting. The little girl's nursery was complete with an expensive layette and a sterling silver rattle. Employees at the Matchless Mine sent the child a gold-lined cup, saucer, and spoon. Horace sent small gold medallions to many of Denver's most prominent citizens to announce the birth of his daughter.

Regardless of the opulent living conditions and numerous attempts to obtain good standing in the social community, Baby and Horace were for the most part ostracized. Unable to find grace and acceptance within Denver's elite, Baby decided to focus solely on Horace and his mining claims. The Matchless Mine earned the Tabors more than $1 million annually and his other investments made more than $4 million. Horace used a substantial portion of the family's income to support the Republican Party in Colorado. He had hoped the hefty contribution would help him win a nomination for governor. Baby was frustrated with the treatment he received from the party, which in her opinion had no intentions of placing his name on the ticket. "They took his money and denied him any recognition," Baby lamented.

In his quest to become a man of unlimited power, Horace invested in mines in New Mexico, Arizona, Texas, and Latin America. He purchased forestland in Honduras and he and Baby spent $2 million developing the property. Many of his risky ventures, including the Honduras project, lost millions. In 1888 the Tabors had a son who lived only a few hours after his birth. Their second daughter was born in December 1889.

Ten years after Horace and Baby were wed, the bottom fell out of the silver market and overnight the Tabors lost all the wealth

Baby Doe Tabor, once the wife of millionaire Horace Tabor, dressed like a pauper in her later years. Residents of Denver, Colorado, pass by the miner as she scuttles along the sidewalk wearing a shabby long skirt, overcoat, scarf, and hat.

they had accumulated. "It seems incredible that it should have all happened so quickly," Baby later recalled, "but with one stroke of President Cleveland's pen, establishing the demonetization of silver, all of our mines, and particularly the Matchless, were worthless."

The Tabors were stripped of their possessions a little at a time over a six-month period. By December 1893, all that remained of their vast fortune was the Matchless Mine, and even that had to be shut down because the market would not support its yield. At sixty-three years old, Horace went to work as a regular laborer at a mine he had once owned. Baby tried to manage the minimal funds her husband brought in and cared for their two daughters.

With the Tabors unable to pay their electric and water bill, workmen came to the house to shut off their utilities. Baby was livid. "Just wait until Congress repeals the ridiculous law about the regulation of silver and the Matchless is running again," she told the workmen. "Then you'll be sorry you acted like this."

The Tabors moved into a small home on the west side of town. Denver's socialites gossiped about Horace and Baby's relationship, speculating on its longevity now that Horace was broke. Baby heard the rumors and insisted to all who would listen that she and Horace would stay together through the difficulties and rebuild their lives on the renewed success of the Matchless Mine.

According to Baby Doe, in late February 1898, she met with Colorado Senator Ed Wolcott and pleaded with him to help her and her family. Wolcott knew Baby from her days in Central City and Leadville, and he and Horace had squared off politically on several occasions. It was due to Senator Wolcott's efforts that Horace was appointed as Denver's postmaster. The job paid $3,500 a year and helped restore a modicum of dignity to Horace's life. Baby was overjoyed. She believed it was an indication that their luck had changed and that their old life would soon be restored. But harder times were yet to come.

On April 3, 1899, Horace died from an acute appendicitis attack. Baby was at his side when he passed away. With his last breath he encouraged his wife to hold on to the Matchless Mine. Cards and letters of condolence poured in from national and state political leaders. Flags across Colorado were ordered to be flown at half-mast. Thousands of mourners lined Denver's streets to see Horace's funeral procession. After a graveside service, Horace was laid to rest at the Calvary Cemetery. He was later moved to the Mount Olive Cemetery when the Calvary Cemetery was dissolved.

With Horace gone, the grief-stricken Baby decided to focus her efforts on finding investors to back the reopening of the Matchless Mine. Having been unworked for many years, the mine was filled with water and initial funds were needed to pump the liquid out, stabilize the tunnels, and purchase new machinery. After an exhaustive search Baby located a businessman who fronted her the capital to begin operations. Baby moved her fifteen- and nine-year-old daughters, Elizabeth Lillie and Rose, to Leadville where the Matchless Mine was located, and she went to work hiring help to support the dig. She encouraged her children to learn all the aspects of running the mine, from swinging a pick to hauling ore to the surface, but her eldest daughter refused to ever have any part of it.

When the Matchless Mine failed to produce any significant gold, the investor withdrew his support, forcing Baby to search for other backers. This scenario was repeated time and time again. She refused to give up or sell the property outright, and for three decades she steadfastly maintained that riches were buried deep within the walls of the mine. Her children grew up and moved on, but Baby remained in Colorado in a dilapidated cabin located at the site. "I shall never let the Matchless go," she told a banker she was asking to back the mine operations. "Not while there is a breath in my body to find a way to fight for it."

When the money ran out, Baby worked the mine alone. Occasionally she sold off a few of Horace's valuables (such as watch fobs and cufflinks) to buy food and clothing. Both of her daughters tired of their mother's obsession with the Matchless and distanced themselves from her. Elizabeth Lillie married and moved to Wisconsin; Rose (or "Silver Dollar," as her mother called her) drifted to Chicago where she was murdered at the age of thirty-five. With the exception of a neighbor and benevolent mine engineer and his

Baby Doe Tabor's home at the Matchless Mine where she lived out her final years.

daughter, Baby Doe lived the life of a recluse, visited by no one. The journal she kept in her later days describes how lonely she was and how much she missed Horace and her children. An entry she made on April 19, 1925, reads "Holy Thursday. Dreamed of being with Tabor, Lillie, and Silver and seeing rich ore in No. 6 shaft."

In 1932, a movie entitled *Silver Dollar* about the life and career of Horace Tabor premiered in Denver, Colorado. It generated new interest in the Tabor legacy and in his affair with Baby Doe. Press agents and historians sought out Baby to interview her and persuade her to tell her story in exchange for a fee, but she refused. She maintained that the Matchless Mine would ultimately supply any money worth making.

On February 20, 1935, Baby Doe Tabor, the woman once known throughout the West as the "Silver Queen," died. A severe blizzard blanketed Leadville with snow and ice, and Baby, who was suffering from pneumonia, was unable to keep a fire going in her cabin. Her neighbors became concerned about her when they didn't see any smoke emanating from the chimney. Her frozen body was found lying on the floor of her rundown cabin, her arms outstretched at her sides.

Funeral services for Baby Doe were held at a church in Leadville, and her remains were then taken to Denver to be buried next to Horace. The headline across the front of the *Rocky Mountain* newspaper read "Baby Doe Dies at Her Post Guarding Matchless Mine." The article that followed reported on the squalid conditions of her home and noted that only a "small cache of food and a few sticks of firewood" were found on the premises.

Among the personal belongings she left behind were seventeen trunks filled with a variety of memorabilia including scrapbooks, old newspapers, and a silver Tiffany tea set. Sue Bonnie, the daughter of the mine engineer who called on Baby from 1927 until her death, used Baby Doe's scrapbook and journal entries, along with their documented conversations, to write a series of articles. From January to May in 1938, the articles about Baby Doe and her recollections of life as a miner and her marriage to Horace Tabor were published in *True Story Magazine*.

Baby Doe Tabor was eighty-one years old when she passed away. The one-time heiress to a vast silver empire had remained faithful to her husband's parting advice for thirty-six years.

ELLEN NAY:
FOUNDER OF THE
ELLENDALE MINES

"Oh, Lord, I never supposed there was so much gold in the world!"

—Ellen Nay, April 1909

A thin, unshaven prospector took a long drag off the butt of a cigarette before flopping into an oversized chair in the plush lobby of the Mizpah Hotel in Tonopah, Nevada. The six-story building featured all the conveniences possessed by establishments like it in New York. The rooms and foyer were primarily occupied by stylishly dressed men and women from all walks of life. The scruffy miner held up in the main room looked out of place among the sophisticated clientele, but he didn't seem to mind.

He was waiting for a storm to clear before venturing out of the hotel and into the mountains outlining the town. The downpour that had swept through the area was so sudden and violent that it would have been impossible for the Argonaut to make an ounce of headway. The air was filled with grit and sand and sagebrush flew away like feathers.

The miner snapped open a copy of the *Nevada State Journal* dated Sunday, July 4, 1909, and scanned the news across the page.

His eyes stopped on an article that began "Reports on Another Ellendale Strike." The man leaned forward in his chair, studying the piece with great interest. "A second really great strike occurred yesterday afternoon at Ellendale. In addition to it, various leases on the Mount Ellen lode are getting gold pannings showing that the richness of Ellendale extends for a great and indefinite distance north and south."

The miner quickly folded the newspaper in half and shoved it into a bedroll at his feet. As though suddenly infused with a bolt of energy, he gathered his things and headed for the exit. Pausing long enough only to turn his jacket collar up around his ears, he charged out the door into the downpour and disappeared into a curtain of rain.

The feverish obsession to locate a strike on the richest ground in Nevada in 1909 drove prospectors to the fertile area named for the woman who first discovered gold on the site: Ellen Nay. For a chance at securing a wealthy claim in Ellendale, gold seekers would brave harsh weather and incredibly rough living conditions. Driven by her own desire for gold, Ellen Nay succumbed to the same difficulties. The rich results secured for her a position among a handful of successful women miners in the Old West.

Born on August 29, 1879, in Tybo, Nevada to Scotch-Irish and English immigrant parents, Ellen (or "Ellie" as her family called her) inherited her father's love for prospecting. From the time he was old enough to hold down a job, Edward Clifford had almost exclusively worked as a miner. He began laboring in coalmines in Maryland and Pennsylvania when he was in his teens, then slowly worked his way west through Colorado and Wyoming employed in the same field. Edward moved his wife and children to Nevada in the mid-1870s in search of silver. He taught his eleven children how to read the rocks scattered among the hillsides and to examine the markings in the earth for fragments of iron and gold.

Ellen's father allowed her to accompany him on many of his gold-hunting trips. He was a strong influence in her life, as were the many other miners living in the Tybo community. By 1875, nearly $10 million in silver was extracted from the mines. Tybo was the state's top producer of silver-lead ore. Ellen's education in the field was well rounded and because she aspired to be a prospector, she eagerly learned all she could about the profession.

The Cliffords lived outside of the mining camp on a remote ranch in Stone Cabin Valley. Ellen was a spirited brunette who worked hard at the various chores around the homestead, including tasks most girls didn't do, such as blacksmithing and woodworking. She was as fine a cook as she was a carpenter. She attended a one-room schoolhouse until the age of twelve and spent her play time with her younger brothers and sisters.

Trips to Belmont, the Nye County seat, were special occasions for the Cliffords. The family loaded up on supplies at the local mercantile, and Ellen got a chance to listen in on conversations between the prospectors who owned property in the area. The mines in and around Belmont produced millions in gold and silver, and discussion about the various strikes further encouraged Ellen to one day pursue a claim of her own.

In 1896, during a routine family visit to Belmont, Ellen met a young adventurer-turned-cowboy by the name of Joseph Bringham Nay. (Some newspaper accounts spell Joseph's name Ney.) The twenty-five-year-old man and his brother had left their home in Pine Valley, Utah to see the western territory. They had decided to stay in the mining camp for a few days when he made Ellen's acquaintance. Joe found the seventeen-year-old Ellen extremely charming and he

A sample of the gold ore found on Ellen Nay's mining claim is clutched tightly in her right hand. Her proud husband, Joe, is at her side.

was persuaded to linger in the area a bit longer than planned. He accepted a job herding stray cattle for ranchers in a valley ninety miles away from the Clifford ranch.

After three years of courting, the couple decided to get married. The two were wed on December 7, 1889, in a ceremony attended by most of the Nye County population. The newlyweds divided their time between Ellen's parents' ranch and their own home in Belmont. Joe rounded up cattle and drove them from the Kawich Mountains to the railroad at Silver Peak. The pair had their first child in December 1900. Ellen was twenty-one years old, a wife, and a mother, but the ambition to prospect was as enticing as it had been when she was a girl. News of a substantial gold find in a town several miles north of the Clifford's homestead prompted her to seek her heart's desire.

The Mizpah claim Jim Butler and his wife discovered in August 1900 in the Toyiyabe Mountains surrounding Tonopah had made the town the richest gold camp in Nevada. After Ellen's father ventured to the new mining district in late 1901, he persuaded his daughter to think about doing the same. Ellen spoke with Joseph about the move. He was hesitant at first for two reasons: One was that Ellen was about to give birth to their second child; the second reason was that he knew nothing about mining. Ellen assured him that she knew enough for both of them and that in time he would become an expert prospector. Joseph put his faith in his wife's talent for mining and relocated to the state's new boomtown.

The living conditions the Nays were first exposed to in the frantic and crowded mining camp were primitive. They lived in canvas tents with limited furnishings. Ellen tried to make it a comfortable and warm home. Joseph supported his family by working two jobs, as a cowboy and a digger for another man's claim. In his off hours he and Ellen would comb the area looking for their own parcel to mine. In 1904, however, a complication arose that delayed their chance to secure any land.

An altercation between Joseph and an argumentative cowboy he'd met en route from Utah ended in violence when the pair ran into each other in the streets of Tonopah. The two men decided to settle their long-standing dispute using their guns. Both were seriously injured in the gunfight; Joseph's leg was in danger of being amputated. The Nays' search for gold had to be put on hold until Joseph recovered.

New claims were being struck all around the area where the couple and their two young children lived. Edward Clifford was looking for a fortune in the nearby mining camp of Goldfield, which boasted a population of thirty thousand people and in its heyday produced $11 million in gold. Edward kept his daughter and son-in-law up to date on the richest finds.

Ellen and Joseph rejoined the gold rushers in late 1904. The valuable strikes that had been made around Tonopah had almost all been played out. Like Ellen's father, miners had shifted their attention to Goldfield. Ellen convinced Joseph they needed to move. Although he was still recovering from his gunshot wound, he agreed. Once they reached Goldfield, Joseph found work as a laborer at a local mine. Ellen supplemented their income by taking in laundry. By April 1905, the two had saved enough money to invest in quality mining equipment, pack animals, and provisions for a trip into the mountains around Goldfield.

The Nays began their search for gold fifty miles east of Goldfield at the southern edge of the Kawich Range. Carrying two baby girls with them on their journey, Joseph and Ellen pushed their way past jagged rocks and inched their way along mountainous caverns they hoped would lead to a fortune. By January 1906, each of them had staked out claims for themselves.

The potential for untold wealth was great, but mining life was hard, especially on children. Ellen suggested they find a spot somewhere between their claims and Goldfield to build a house and a mercantile. The Nays decided to settle in an area near the Sugarloaf Mountains, where they had been mining and already owned property on a spot called Salsbury Walsh.

Many of the claims in the Salsbury Walsh area that had been discovered and moderately worked dated back to 1900. The miners who initially dug on the location chose to abandon the area and head off to richer prospects in Goldfield and Tonopah. Ellen believed there was still some value in those deserted claims.

The Nays opened the door to their Salsbury Walsh stage stop in 1909. Packers, prospectors, and pioneers passing through the area visited the small roadhouse where they could purchase various supplies and food. Ellen's mother and father watched the store and her girls while she and Joseph looked for gold. They searched for months but found nothing. "I was feeling tired and discouraged," Ellen wrote in her journal the morning she made her rich strike. "I told Joe to do the panning and I would go out and bring in more float."

It was late in the afternoon on the 31st of March 1909 that the Nays' back-breaking efforts proved to be worthwhile. Ellen later recalled:

> When we got back to my claim it was about 4 o'clock in the afternoon. I stayed up the wash a ways and found a boulder half hidden in the sand. I knocked off a little piece, examined it, and found a pretty speck of gold. I knocked off a larger piece, and my gracious, it was half covered with yellow stuff that looked like gold, but I couldn't believe my eyes. I threw off my bonnet and away I flew to Joe. I told him I couldn't believe it was gold—there was too much of it. I never saw so much gold on a single piece of rock before. But Joe insisted it was gold and he, too, began to get excited. He wanted to know if there was any more of it and I told him the rock was too big for me to carry. Joe forgot all about being lame, and away we went. I wrapped the boulder up in my apron and Joe carried it. It weighed seventy-five pounds and was just full of gold.

Neither Joe nor Ellen slept much the first night after the discovery. They were anxious to trace the lead back to the original source. The couple elicited the help of their families to find the main gold-bearing vein, promising to share the wealth with them when it was found.

Joseph's brother used a mining hammer to tap his way through the rich ledge. Ellen and her father did the same from the other side, using picks. When the group located the vein they shouted for joy. Twenty-nine-year-old Ellen had finally become the successful prospector she'd always dreamed of being.

Ellen's father and husband assumed control of the dig. A claim was filed on Ellen's discovery six months after she found the massive nugget. The reason for the long passage of time was so that the Nays and Cliffords could develop the strike; they wanted to plot out areas around and on the find to be sold off in an orderly fashion. News of a strike at the site would generate a rush of people to the area and increase the potential for claim jumping. When all the plots for the town, aptly named Ellendale, were laid out, the public was made aware of the gold discovery.

The July 20, 1909, edition of the *Nevada State Journal* carried an article about the Ellendale Mines and estimated that the initial shipment from the southern portion of the camp was valued at $20,000:

> The *Tonopah Bonanza* says that while the exact returns of the ore shipped from the original strike at Ellendale have not been given out, it is stated that it will return in the neighborhood of $4,200 per ton net.
>
> In the shipment there were exactly five tons, which shows a valuation of over $20,000. Yesterday Mr. Warburton was seen by representatives of the Bonanza concerning the value of the ore that was taken to Millers. He said that he was not in a position to give out any authentic information, but that it was known

Many miners in the gold mining town of Tonopah, Nevada, abandoned their prospects in the area in favor of working the rich diggings in Ellendale.

the ore would run between $4,000 and $5,000 to the ton. He said that the consignment weighed just exactly five tons. No word has yet been received from the umpire assays that were being made at Hasen, consequently there was no check on the assays which had been made by the Western Ore Purchasing Company at Millers.

At any rate the shipment shows that the new camp of Ellendale is a producer of high-grade gold ore. It remains now for the leasers to open up ore bodies to prove the continuity of the rich lead and from indications at the present time there is every reason to believe that it is but the matter of a very short time until a steady stream of gold ore will be sent from the camp.

The shipment has created no unrest in Ellendale. The people have been more than anxious to learn its value. That it came up to their expectations goes without saying. It is not every day in the mining world that ore of such richness is found upon the surface and proves that there are opportunities for the prospector in Southern Nevada unexcelled in any part of the country. The field is still wide, having been no more than scratched.

Eager buyers purchased lots for as much as $550. By August the town was booming, businesses and homes were constructed, and miners were burrowing into the earth. Rumors that the gold initially found there was only a surface discovery stalled growth for a bit, but a report in the August 19, 1909, edition of the *Nevada State Journal* refuted the claim. "The main strike is bigger and richer than ever," the article read. "It is looking great. Pannings are now being secured in the tunnel at the main strike and it looks like the ledge was not far away."

Ellen was proud of the community that grew up around her strike. She gave tours of the grounds to reporters and prospective investors and welcomed anyone into her home who wanted to know more about her life as a mother, wife, and miner. She was recognized by Ellendale citizens as the "uncrowned queen" of the camp.

For a time thousands of dollars worth of gold were extracted from Ellen Nay's find, but by November 1909, the area had been completely played out. Ellen refused to believe all the value had been dug out of the property and continued to prospect in the vicinity even after all the camp followers had left the scene.

The Nays used the profits from Ellen's discovery to purchase a ranch outside of Belmont. The horses and cattle roamed the land around the idyllic homestead, which possessed a beautiful view of

Mount Jefferson. Ellen enjoyed life at the Barley Creek ranch, but her interest in mining never wavered. Her collection of ore samples was prominently displayed in her home and she eagerly discussed any finds made by the handful of hopeful prospectors who leased land in Ellendale.

Two small bonanzas—one in 1913 and the other in 1930—supported Ellen's conviction that there was more gold to be found in Ellendale. Throughout the years, she and Joseph would make trips into the all but deserted mining camp and work the claim themselves. Their daughters and eventually their daughters' husbands participated in the search for another rich strike. No other find equaled Ellen's original discovery.

In the spring of 1939, Ellen suffered a major loss: Joseph, her husband and mining partner for more than forty years, died of a heart attack.

She sold the ranch where they had lived for many years and moved to Fallon with one of her daughters. On April 2, 1947, Ellen was attending to some mining business in Tonopah when she became ill. She was quickly rushed to the hospital where she died of heart failure.

News of Ellen's passing was carried in every major paper in Nevada. She was remembered as a "pioneer and an expert mineralogist who discovered the rich 'Ellendale' mine." The April 4, 1947, edition of the *Tonopah Times Bonanza* reported that the "news of her death came as a sudden shock to the many people in the area that had valued her friendship. It falls to few persons that live on this earth that the great good fortune to be held so dear in the hearts and minds of so many friends as was Mrs. Ellen Nay."

DAME SHIRLEY:
MINER ON THE FEATHER RIVER

"I shall give you a full, true, and particular account of the discovery, rise, and progress of this place, with a religious adherence to dates which will rather astonish your unmathematical mind."

—Excerpt from Louise Clappe's letter to
her sister Mary Ann, September 20, 1851

The sun hung like a golden disc in an impossible blue sky over the primitive trail leading to the gold camp of Rich Bar in northern California. The wind swirled over the lush green landscape tossing wildflower petals into the air and creating ripples across the surface of the clear waters of the Feather River. Louise Clappe, a young pioneer bride, rode through the tranquil setting beside a bearded driver in his supply-laden wagon. She let her eyes drift to the ruggedness beyond where the snow-covered Sierra mountain peaks cut sharply into the sky and wispy clouds drifted around the summit.

The vehicle came to a complete stop. Louise glanced inquisitively at the driver and he casually nodded toward a band of Native Americans blocking the roadway and eyeing the travelers carefully. Little by little more filtered out from behind the trees and brush surrounding the wagon.

They were friendly people, more curious than threatened by the invaders on their land. The women gently approached Louise and the wagon to get a closer look. The infants they carried in their arms cooed and wriggled happily. The men watched their wives and daughters touch Louise's clothing and stroke her hat and shoes in wonder.

Louise was moved by their peaceful scrutiny and fascinated with their looks as well. She opened the handbag resting in her lap and produced a package of straight pins. She placed one of the pins into the hand of a young woman dressed in a thigh-length skirt of rushes pounded into threads and tied about the hips. The woman smiled brightly and turned to the others around her to show off the treasure she had just received. Without a moment's hesitation the remainder of the women in the group as well as the men extended their hands to the benevolent Mrs. Clappe. They all hoped that they would be given a gift too.

Louise captured the moving encounter with the Indians as well as the details and spirit of her journey to the gold fields in a series of letters written to her sister living in the East. Her firsthand description of a unique place and time during the gold rush is considered by most historians to be as valuable as the nuggets found in California's streams and mines.

Born in 1819 in Amherst, Massachusetts, Louise Amelia Knapp-Smith was an orphan. She learned to read and write at an early age, and by the time she was nineteen years old she was a published author. Her talent for writing was nurtured by a distinguished diplomat named Alexander Hill Everett. The pair met in Massachusetts and when Everett took a job as a U.S. Commissioner in China, he and Louise began writing letters back and forth. Alexander was a well-known writer and encouraged Louise to hone her craft. "If," he wrote, "you would add to your love of reading the habit of writing, you would find a new and inexhaustible source of comfort and satisfaction opening upon you."

Louise took her mentor's advice and penned a number of short stories that served as practical experience for the work yet to come. She created a clear, straightforward style unlike the literary work common at the time by writers like Sarah Orne Jewett and Louisa May Alcott.

Armed with a desire to see the West and recount the sights and sounds to her adopted sister, Mary Ann (referred to in her letters as Molly), Louise traveled to California with her husband, Dr. Fayette Clappe. The petite, vivacious blonde arrived in San Francisco in 1849. After two winters in the fog, wind, and cold of San Francisco, the inclement weather became too much for the physician to tolerate. On the recommendation of a friend, he decided to go to Rich Bar near the crest of the Sierras on Feather River.

In the spring of 1851, Dr. Clappe sent for his wife and she enthusiastically began packing. Her friends thought the move was a bad idea. One friend suggested, "It was indelicate to go alone among so many men." Louise politely thanked them for their concern and proceeded to the gold fields anyway. Shortly after reaching the mines, she began sending letters to her sister describing the coarse and often brutal nature of life in the mining camps. She wrote a total of twenty-three letters, which were later published in a literary magazine called *The Pioneer* under Louise's pen name, Dame Shirley.

In her first letter, Louise posed a question she suspected Mary Ann would ask. "How did such a frail, home-loving little thistle ever float safely to that faraway spot; and take root so kindly . . . in that barbarous soil? And, for pity's sake, how does the poor little fool expect to amuse herself there?"

Louise's account of her journey shows the spirit that prevails throughout her letters. Passing quickly over the boring steamboat ride upriver, she began her story at the rancho ten miles below Marysville. Here her husband met her; most of her clothes were left to be transported later. Rich Bar could be reached only by mule train. Louise wrapped a few toilet articles in a sheet, which was tied to the back of a mule. She described the beauty of the distant buttes as they traveled to Marysville. There were no sidesaddles, but Louise thought it amusing to ride astride.

Her first adventure happened shortly after they set out. The saddle was too large for the mule. It slipped sideways, dumping Louise into the dust. Dr. Clappe suggested that they return so Louise could change clothes, but she refused. The doctor, fearful of another accident, walked the spindly-legged mule to Marysville. They arrived at midnight. The hotel help had gone to bed; the only refreshments available were dried apple pies, cheese, and "those tempting and saw dustiest of luxuries, crackers." Louise wanted something hot. Dr. Clappe went out to a restaurant and ordered a meal: hot oysters, toast, tomatoes, and coffee. She finished them gratefully and fell asleep.

The stage from Marysville to Bidwell Bar was, Louise wrote, "the most excruciatingly springless wagon that it was ever my lot to be victimized in." Her husband went ahead by mule, so she was alone. The road was steep and narrow. Cliffs crowded in on one side, a "yawning chasm" on the other. "Wonder to relate," she wrote, "I did not oh! Or ah! Nor shriek once." After they crossed the last mountain the Welsh driver complimented her. He said she was "the fust woman that ever come over that 'ere mount'in without hollerin'." Louise was ashamed to admit that fear had kept her mute.

Dr. Clappe met his wife at Bidwell Bar. "There was," she wrote, "only a tent to sleep in, only the ground to sleep on." The air was black with fleas. In the night a grizzly bear came "shuffling about." Louise was frightened, but her husband, awakened by her whisper, simply turned over and went back to sleep.

After two days and nights of traveling through the wilderness alone, a miner escorted the couple on to Rich Bar. Dr. Clappe and Louise checked into the Empire Hotel, a framed structure with starched calico and blue drill stretched about four walls. The inside walls of the upstairs rooms were white cotton. But there were voluminous curtains at the glass windows, which were brought in from Marysville by mules. The first floor contained a saloon and bowling alley. Louise soon learned that next to cards, bowling was the miners' chief recreation.

In a letter dated September 20, 1851, Louise conveyed her impressions of the mining camp outside of the hotel and her husband's makeshift office.

Imagine a tiny valley about eight hundred yards in length, and perhaps thirty in width (it was measured for my especial information), apparently hemmed in by lofty hills, almost perpendicular, draperied to their very summits with beautiful fir trees, the blue-bosomed Plumas (or Feather River, I suppose I must call it) undulating along their base—and you have as good an idea as I can give you of the local Barra Rica, as the Spaniards so prettily term it. In almost any of the numerous books written upon California, no doubt you will be able to find a most scientific description of the origin of these bars. I must acknowledge with shame that my ideas on the subject are distressingly vague. I could never appreciate the poetry or

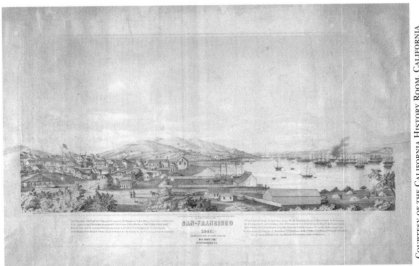

Women gold rushers arriving in San Francisco in 1849 found the city by the bay crowded with hopeful prospectors scrambling to reach the mother lode before anyone else could get to it.

the humor of making one's wrists ache by knocking to pieces gloomy-looking stones, or in dirtying one's fingers by analyzing soils, in a vain attempt to fathom the osteology or anatomy of our beloved earth, though my heart is thrillingly alive to the faintest shade of color and the infinite variety of styles in which she delights to robe her ever-changeful and ever-beautiful surface."

Dr. Clappe referred to his office as "a perfect marvel to the miners, from its superior elegance." Louise was anxious to see this marvel. As she stepped into the log building, she saw two ten-foot-long benches along either side of the dirt-floored room. A small window was covered with white cotton, a rude sign on it declaring his profession.

Medicines and medical books were displayed on crude shelves resembling "sticks snatched from the wood pile." The walls were adorned with pictures cut from *Godey's Ladies' Book,* a fashion magazine of the day, and from *Graham's* and *Sartain's* magazines for men. The figures looked, she wrote, like "imaginary monsters, sporting miraculous waists, impossible wrists and fabulous feet."

Louise was proud of her husband and eagerly accepted his invitation for her to help him with his practice. Louise and Fayette traveled on pack mules to call on patients in the outlying areas. In the spring of 1852, they attended to a young miner who had been critically injured in an accident.

A few days prior, a rolling boulder crushing the prospector's leg had unearthed $4,000 in gold. After Dr. Clappe amputated the man's leg, typhoid fever set in. Louise sat with the miner, wiping his brow and talking with him until he died. "On the evening of his death," Louise wrote her sister, "he sat up, opened his eyes, and whispered, "Do you hear the funeral procession returning?"

"How oddly do life and death jostle each other in this strange world of ours!" Louise lamented to Molly.

The cloth walls that surrounded Louise and Fayette's hotel room could not prevent her from hearing the profanity that the miners constantly used. Some of their expressions, she wrote, "were they not so fearfully blasphemous, would be grotesquely sublime." She explained that the loneliness of being away from loved ones caused them to drink and swear far more than they would have at home.

The cloth walls also made it hard to sleep, for the noise was always with her. Miners came in at all hours, shouting and singing. The bowling alley was never quiet, day or night. Mining equipment rattled and squeaked far into the night. There was a dog nearby that barked at all hours. Added to this was the noise of the wooden flume, hung

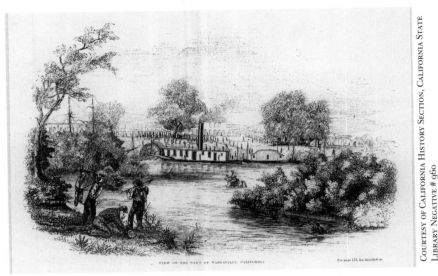

Marysville, California, as it looked when Louise Clappe passed through in 1849.

by chains from the canyon walls to carry water to the sluices. Louise described its sound as "resembling those of a suffering child."

Although there were certain crude aspects to living in a mining camp, Louise was amused by the hell-roaring life surrounding her. The methods employed by prospectors to attract the attention of the few females living in the area or passing through was of particular interest to her. "To impress a lady," she wrote, "they salt their diggings. The dear creatures go home with their treasures, firmly believing that mining is the prettiest pastime in the world."

After spending six months in Rich Bar, Dr. Clappe decided he and Louise should move farther downriver to a spot called Indian Bar. A bigger find of gold had been discovered at the location. A doctor's services were in great need there and they could name their own price. Dr. Clappe, as well as any other physician, was paid in gold nuggets. He believed the move to Indian Bar would be personally and financially rewarding.

The Clappes arrived in Indian Bar in October 1851. They were greeted by a large homemade United States flag. A sailor had climbed to the top of a fir tree, fastened the flag, and removed the branches as he descended; it had been there since the Fourth of July.

The hotel was another "rag shanty" of white cotton and blue drill; the sign above the entrance read Humboldt Hotel. The hotel had something unusual: In the bar/dancehall there was a wooden floor. There was also the ubiquitous bowling alley.

The canyon was so narrow that they were unable to reach their cabin except by going through the hotel's kitchen. There Louise met Paganini Ned, the cook who was also chief fiddler in the dancehall. The frame-and-canvas door hung open. "Enter my dear, you are welcome," she was told. "Besides, we could not keep you out if we would, as there is no latch on the door." The cabin was about twenty feet square, divided into two rooms by an unhemmed curtain. The ceiling was white cotton, sewn together in spots so that, wrote Louise, "it hung gracefully open, giving one a bird's-eye view of the shingles above."

The wooden floor was so uneven that "the chairs, tables, etc., remind you constantly of a dog with a sore foot." The walls were hung with chintz, the pattern of wreathed roses in brown, purple, green, and yellow. A log settee leaned against a wall. A small, square chess table was covered with oilcloth. Candle boxes made a bookcase. The fireplace was of rocks and mud, with an inside chimney of sticks and mud. The mantel was a log covered with flattened tin cans, the gaily painted labels advertising various canned fruits.

In the bedroom, trunks or claret boxes were dressers. A mining pan was a washbowl. The bedstead was so massive that "in ponderousness it leaves the Empire couches far behind." The small window had no covering; glass could not come from Marysville till spring. Louise declared, however, that she was just as happy. She had always enjoyed sitting beside an open window, even in the winter.

But the biggest surprise was the long dining table. It was set with a white cloth and napkins were beside the plates and glasses. And Paganini Ned stood resplendent in a new blue flannel shirt and blue pants, ready to serve a dinner in her honor. The menu: oyster soup, fried salmon (from the river), roast beef and boiled ham, fried oysters, boiled potatoes and onions, mince pie and pudding (without eggs or milk), nuts and raisins, claret, champagne, and coffee. Of the coffee, Louise wrote that "Ned must have got the recipe for making it from the very angel who gave the beverage to Mahomet." Ned served the meal with a grand air and ceremony. "It was one of those scenes," Louise mused, "just touched with that fine and almost imperceptive perfume of the ludicrous."

In late 1852, when the mines were failing and crime was on the increase, Louise and her husband returned to San Francisco. Dr. Clappe opened another practice and Louise turned to teaching. In 1854, the restless Fayette decided to return to the mining camps and when he had not been heard from for three years, Louise filed for divorce. Her health began to fail in 1878 and she moved to New York to live with her niece. She earned her living delivering lectures on art and literature.

In 1897, Louise entered a home for the elderly and remained there until her death on February 11, 1906, at the age of eighty-seven. Among the prized possessions found in her room were the letters that Alexander Everett had written to her more than seventy years earlier. The "Shirley Letters" have become classic reading for those interested in the early mining days of California.

NELLIE CASHMAN:
TOUGHEST OF THE
LADY SOURDOUGHS

"She had beauty without ostentation, wisdom without education, and a flaming unquenchable spirit that was nonetheless familiar with the paths of true humility."

—*Arizona Daily Star,* January 12, 1925

Night had fallen over Tombstone, Arizona, and every restless and rowdy character in the vicinity of the southwestern town had poured into the saloons and gambling dens to while away the hours until dawn arrived. The doorways of the numerous taverns that lined Allen Street were illuminated with smoky kerosene torches. Signs that hung over the entrances to the rowdy buildings sported such names as the Occidental, the Oriental, and the Bird Cage Opera House; they swayed back and forth in the dusty wind. Music, laughter, the sound of a gambler rejoicing in a win, and the occasional pistols firing spilled out of the dance halls into the street and drifted into the starlit sky.

Nellie Cashman, a dark-eyed Irish beauty with ebony curls fashioned into a bun, fixed a determined gaze toward the town's main thoroughfare. She stepped out of her restaurant, the Russ House at

Fifth and Toughnut Street, and strolled across the boardwalk to a hitching post.

The usual gunfire in the near distance was nothing to be concerned about. "Just another drunken cowboy feeling fearless," she told herself out loud. A disheveled, bearded prospector wearing tattered clothes and a faded flop hat exited the eatery and walked over to Nellie. "You ain't worried about those shots are you?" he asked. "Not unless they get closer to my place," she said half smiling. The elderly miner gave his belly a satisfied pat and breathed in the desert air. "You know," he began, "all Tombstone needs to be the garden spot of the world is more good people like yourself and water." Nellie listened for the echo of more gunfire, but none came. "Well, stranger," she finally replied. "I reckon that's all Hades needs too."

The prospector gathered up his things and thanked her for the fine meal. "The Russ House is open to everyone, even if you don't have any money," she assured him. "Come back any time." The miner tipped his hat, waved goodbye, and disappeared into the night, pulling his pack mule behind him. He wasn't the first destitute frontiersman who had benefited from Nellie's kindness and he wouldn't be the last.

Nellie moved to the wild burg of Tombstone in 1880 for the same reason hundreds of other ambitious fortune seekers did: to mine for gold. She had been searching for the glittery substance for years prior to her stay in the town yet to be made famous by the Gunfight at the O.K. Corral. Convinced that she would one day hit the mother lode, Nellie followed stampedes from Montana to Arizona. When she wasn't prospecting she operated boardinghouses and restaurants. "Looking for nuggets is like hunting for a whisper in a big wind," she reminded friends and family. "You have to have an occupation to fall back on while you're searching for a strike."

Nellie's businesses offered miners a clean place to call home and appetizing meals. Her hotels were always crowded, and if a man had no money, Nellie would provide board and lodging until he made a stake; she would even loan him the money to find that stake. In 1908, the *Alaska Fairbanks Daily News* described the tenacious, benevolent woman as "hard as flint, with endurance on the trail equal to that of any man, but with an inexhaustible fund of good humor and a cheery word and a helping hand for anyone in need."

Ellen Cashman was born in Queenstown, County Cork, Ireland in 1850. For most of Nellie's upbringing her native country had languished in a state of depression. Food and jobs were hard to come by. Her father passed away at an early age trying to provide for his family, which consisted of his wife Frances and daughters Nellie and Fanny. At the age of seventeen and with hopes of securing a better future, Nellie made the trip across the ocean to America with her widowed mother and her sister. The trio landed in Boston on May 12, 1867. Both Nellie and Frances quickly found work at the popular hotels around the harbor. Nellie was employed as a bellhop (a job ordinarily occupied by a young man, but the Civil War had left few men to do such work) at an establishment where General Ulysses S. Grant frequently stayed. During one of his visits he met the hard-working girl and offered advice about her future pursuits. "He was easy to talk to," Nellie recalled to a newspaper reporter in early 1900, "like everyone I ever knew. When I told him I wanted to do things, because I had to if I wanted to live, he said, "Why don't you go West, young woman? The West needs people like you.""

Nellie took the future president's words to heart and in late 1869, she and her sister and mother boarded a train bound for San Francisco, a city overrun with people from all walks of life. In the

Born in Queenstown, County Cork, Ireland, Nellie Cashman was the quintessential American pioneer. As well as being a gold prospector, she was a philanthropist and entrepreneur.

twenty years since gold had been discovered at Captain Sutter's Mill, less than 120 miles from the bustling city, San Francisco had grown from a scruffy camp of tents and log cabins to a booming metropolis that featured three-story stone buildings, ornately built theatres, and stores and shops of every kind. Nellie was excited about the possibilities inherent in the City by the Bay and set about securing a job at once.

Nellie and her sister were well received by the city's predominately male population. Offers of marriage were received on a daily basis. Fanny accepted a proposal from a fellow Irish immigrant, Thomas Cunningham, and the two quickly married. Nellie believed her destiny was in the gold fields and set off to find her fortune.

During her stay in San Francisco, Nellie had heard rumors of a rich strike in Virginia City, Nevada, called the Comstock; she decided to venture to the location. In addition to gold, the hills around the mining camp were lined with silver. More than thirty thousand people resided in Virginia City and its surrounding communities. The boisterous town's saloons and brothels were busy twenty-four hours a day. Cooks were at a premium, and good cooks could make a profitable living. Nellie took full advantage of that fact and opened a short-order restaurant.

When she wasn't preparing simple meals for the hungry miners she was doing her own prospecting. She had a natural gift for digging and panning and managed to collect a substantial amount of gold. As a shrewd businesswoman, she invested her findings in restaurants and boardinghouses in other Nevada mining camps. Nellie also used her financial gain to help others. In her own words, "My goal was to make a lot of money and help anyone who needed it."

Like most ambitious miners, Nellie was willing to relocate to any area where gold was in abundance. She would linger in a given mining camp long enough to see the initial strike decline and then move on. In 1873, after three years of prospecting in Comstock and Pioche, Nevada, Nellie went looking for the heavy yellow rock in British Columbia. Making her home near the town of Victoria, she panned for gold in the Stikine River. Her presence in the remote area earned her the distinction of being the first white woman to live and work in the harsh, seldom-traveled wilderness.

Nellie labored diligently alongside male prospectors in mountainous creek beds and streams that flowed into the Stikine River. She was outspoken and direct and her fellow miners respected her. She would not tolerate any improper sexual advances and was not afraid to stand up to any man who dared cross the line. She never asked to be treated differently from any other miner. She constructed her own sluice and rocker boxes to sift the sand away from the gold, chopped her own wood, and hauled water back and forth to her camp. When asked by an *Arizona Daily Star* reporter in a 1923 interview if she had ever been tempted to use her "feminine wiles" to make life easier, she responded with an emphatic no. "Some women . . . think they should be given special favors because of their sex. Well, all I can say is that those special favors spell doom to a woman and her business. . . . I've paid my bills and played the game like a man."

Cashman's efforts in the Cassair District proved to be rewarding. She retrieved enough gold to fund the purchase of a boardinghouse in Victoria. As usual, the combination hotel and dining hall was always available to customers who did not have the means to pay for food and lodging. Those who could afford her hospitality were asked to contribute what they could to help the Sisters of St. Anne build a hospital. By the winter of 1876, she had raised more than $500. The funds were given to the nuns and construction on St. Joseph's Hospital began the following spring.

Nellie's devotion to the mining party she migrated to British Columbia with was strong. Trappers and lone prospectors passing through her establishment kept her up to date on the health and welfare of the group during her absence from the gold field. When she received news that the men were suffering from scurvy, she loaded supplies and prescribed remedies onto a pack mule and trekked into the mountains. Six woodsmen and trappers accompanied her.

"It took seventy-seven days to reach camp as the winter was very severe," Nellie recalled in a newspaper interview. "At (Fort) Wrangle the United States customs officers tried to dissuade me from taking what they termed 'my mad trip' and, in fact, when we had been several days up the river on our journey they sent up a number of men to induce me to turn back." Nellie's heroic efforts saved the lives of more than seventy ailing miners and earned her the nickname the "Angel of the Cassiar."

In 1879, Nellie returned to the States and was immediately drawn to a fledgling boomtown in the southern Arizona territory. Tucson became a vibrant desert community the minute the Southern Pacific Railroad finished laying tracks through the desert landscape. Nellie believed that a restaurant would be a logical and profitable business to start in the growing pueblo, and shortly after she arrived she turned the idea into a reality. When she opened the doors of her eatery, the Delmonico Restaurant, she became the first single white businesswoman in the area. In an ad placed in the *Arizona Citizen* newspaper, Nellie promised patrons "the best meals in the city," and the popularity of the establishment was proof that her cooking lived up to the bold claims.

The quest for gold and silver lured Nellie away from Tucson within months of the Delmonico's grand opening. News that prospector Ed Schiefflin had discovered silver in a mining camp called Tombstone sent her running to the location. She used the money from the sale of the restaurant in Tucson to invest in a pair of chophouses and a mercantile that sold groceries, ladies' fineries, boots, and shoes.

When Nellie wasn't working at her store or overseeing the operations at her eateries, she was searching the hills around Tombstone for silver ore. Her initial finds were modest but satisfying. As she had done in every place she had made her home, she was involved in charitable work. She was generous to the indigent, hospitals, and the arts, and she helped raise money for a schoolhouse and the building of a church. When she became too busy with community activities to mine herself, she grubstaked mining expeditions, asking for a modest percentage of the find as repayment.

Nellie's kindness and desire to help people extended beyond so-called "polite society" and included assisting prostitutes and prisoners. She provided for any "soiled dove" who lacked food, clothing, and the means to return home to their families. She also made regular visits to death row inmates interned at the Tombstone jail.

The men awaiting execution were alone and fearful of the vengeful residents in the area. Angry citizens had warned the desperados that after they were hung their bodies would be exhumed and dissected. Nellie buoyed the spirits of repentant men by speaking with them about faith in God and promising that their graves would not be disturbed.

The spectacle of public hangings disgusted Nellie. She abhorred the fact that tickets were issued to attend such events and she made her opinions known to local officials. She proved how unafraid she was of interjecting herself in situations she believed were wrong too: When a group of miners wanted to lynch mine owner E.B. Gage, she drove her horse-drawn buggy into the center of the conflict and rescued Gage from the violent crowd.

In the midst of her financial and business triumphs in Tombstone, Nellie experienced personal tragedy. Her beloved sister Fannie and brother-in-law died of tuberculosis, leaving behind five children. Nellie took the orphans in and raised them as her own. All the children achieved success in their lives; her nephew, Michael Cunningham, who as a seven-year-old boy witnessed the Gunfight at the O.K. Corral in October 1881, became president of a bank in Bisbee, Arizona.

No matter how busy Nellie was at the time with the children or the restaurant, she never lost sight of her vision to be a miner. When she learned there was gold to be had in southern California and northern Mexico, she organized an expedition of twenty-one mining experts to accompany her to the region. The prospectors arrived in Guaymas, Mexico on May 24, 1883. Their search led them to the desolate area called Golo Valley. Legend maintains that Nellie happened onto a rich vein of gold in the mountains surrounding the arid basin she called Cashman's Mine, but a priest persuaded her to keep the discovery a secret out of fear that the simple way of life of the indigenous people would be jeopardized and possibly destroyed by a gold rush.

In fact, Nellie and the other miners nearly lost their lives on foot in the hot, sandy desert valley. They had underestimated the amount of provisions necessary to make the journey, and the heat and lack of water was nearly the death of them. It was Nellie's tenacious nature that saved the party. As the healthiest member of the group, she set out on her own to find help. She returned a day later with guides, burros, and goatskins filled with water. The expedition was subsequently cancelled and they made their way back to Tombstone.

In 1886, Nellie sold the Russ House and mercantile, gathered her family together, and for a brief time wandered the mining camps of Wyoming, Montana, and New Mexico. Realizing the vagabond way of life was not the best for her nieces and nephews, she placed them in various Catholic boarding schools in the west. Although the children were not physically with her as they had been, she maintained a close relationship with each one of them and never failed to encourage them in their pursuits or let them know how devoted she was to their happiness and well being.

For ten years Nellie bounced around from mining community to mining community. She owned boardinghouses in Kingston, New Mexico; Coeur d'Alene, Idaho; and Globe, Arizona. During her stay in Globe, she paged through a July 21, 1897, edition of a Phoenix newspaper and read an article about an enormous strike in Alaska. She quickly began making arrangements to explore the Klondike region. An article in the *Arizona Daily Citizen* on September 15, 1897, announced her intentions to leave the southwest.

Nellie calculated that a fully equipped expedition to the Yukon would cost $5,000. She hoped to assemble a six-man team of like-minded miners and trackers to go along with her. All attempts to raise the funds for the trip or attract interested parties to accompany her failed, but it did not stop Nellie from making the journey. On February 15, 1898, she reached Skagway, Alaska. She was determined to travel the perilous Chilkoot Pass to the gold fields.

Dressed in an outfit befitting a Klondike miner and hauling ample supplies for the exploration, the feisty prospector set out to find her bonanza. A newspaper reporter with the *British Colonist* interviewed the fifty-three-year-old woman prior to her departure from the civilized area for the wild countryside. "The first white woman to penetrate the Cassair country and who twenty-one years ago visited Alaska in a quest for gold arrived in the city last night from 'Frisco," the February 1898 article read. "She is out now for a big stake, nothing more or less than the mother lode of the far-framed Klondike region. Miss Cashman is a lithe, active looking woman with jet black hair, and possessed all the vivacity and enthusiasm of a young girl."

Nellie did manage to assemble a small team of men to accompany her and fully expected to be joined by others wanting to go north along the crude mountainous trail. After nearly a three-week trip, Nellie reached the section of wilderness where she would begin panning for gold in the Dyea River and mining in the Rocky Mountains. She filed four claims and worked them all herself. By September 1898, Nellie had recovered more than $100,000 from a claim she called No. 19 Below.

In October, Cashman took a break from prospecting and invested her fortune in a restaurant in Dawson called the Cassair. Half of the facility was used to serve food and the other half was a grocery store. She transformed a portion of the mercantile into a small meeting place for lonely sourdoughs. The miners could sit and enjoy a cup of coffee and a fine cigar while visiting with one another, all of which Nellie offered for free. Her generosity extended to orphaned children, destitute women, and elderly prospectors. She spent tireless hours raising money for hospitals and the building of churches.

In 1899, Nellie experienced another tragedy. Her mother Frances, who had been residing in San Francisco since she and her daughters had moved west in 1869, died. Frances was 101 years old when she passed away and according to the staff at the Magdalen Asylum where she lived, she always spoke fondly of her "adventurous girl, Nellie."

Nellie resided in Dawson for seven years and divided her time between the restaurant, the mercantile, and mining claims. In 1905, she moved her business ventures to Fairbanks. A gold strike on the Chena River near the mining town prompted her to relocate. The drive to find the ultimate strike continued to pull Nellie out of the comfort of her grocery store and eatery and back into the frigid Alaskan hinterlands. At the age of fifty-five, she was recognized as the only female mining expert in the territory. Prospectors frequently sought her advice on where to search for a claim and how to best work the claim after it had been located. Ironically, mining regulations prohibited unmarried women from filing new claims; they could only purchase claims that had already been filed.

Nellie was not resentful about having to work with men to achieve any mining success, nor did she ever worry that a man would take advantage of her. According to a 1923 article in the *Arizona Daily Star*, Nellie was highly complimentary of her male counterparts. "I have mushed with men, slept out in the open, washed with them and been with them constantly, and I have never been offered an insult . . . A woman is safe among miners as at her own fireside. If a woman complains of her treatment from any of the boys, she has only herself to blame . . . I can truthfully say that there was never a bigger hearted class of men than the genuine sourdoughs of Alaska."

From 1907 to 1923, Nellie devoted herself almost entirely to striking it rich. Traveling across the Alaskan territory from the upper Middle Koyukuk River to a camp called Cold Foot, sixty miles from the Artic Circle, she was convinced she would hit it big. The last gold stampede Nellie participated in was at Nolan's Creek at the base of the Brooks Range Mountains. While poking around the jagged bluffs she found a vein of gold that lined the rock under the earth. Getting to the heart of the find required a team of workers, heavy equipment, and even heavier financial backing.

Hoping to attract investors, Nellie formed a corporation called the Midnight Sun Mining Company and immediately began selling stock in the business. She had little difficulty acquiring the initial backing to begin ferreting out the gold. After mining commenced she made frequent trips back to the States to solicit capital to continue operations.

Nellie's fund-raising visits to New York and Washington, D.C., always generated newspaper or magazine articles about her character and vocation. "I've suffered trial and hardships in the frozen plains of Alaska and in the deserts of Arizona," she told a reporter for the *Cordova Alaska Times* in 1917. "I've been alone all my life, but I have been happy and healthy. That's why all are fooled by my age. And that is why I'm not afraid like most women to tell you that I'm sixty-seven and that I'm mighty apt to make a million or two before I leave this romantic business of mining."

No amount of coaxing could entice Nellie to remain with her family after her ventures stateside. She insisted she had to get back to her business in the Alaskan territory, maintaining that she was a "long way from the cushion rocker stage." In 1924, she proved her point when she led a dog-sled team 750 miles over the country's frozen terrain. The feat earned her the title of Champion Woman Musher.

Eight months after the persistent miner accomplished the seventeen-day mushing trip, she came down with a cold that advanced into double pneumonia. The pioneer miner with the benevolent spirit died on January 4, 1925, at St. Joseph's Hospital in Victoria and was laid to rest next to her sister at Ross Bay Cemetery.

GERTRUDE PECKWITH: PROSPECTOR AT THE GOLDEN EMPIRE MINE

"I had worried many times that Mrs. Peckwith would fall from the trail . . . "

—Testimony from Leta Ketcham,
eyewitness to the events leading up to the
death of Gertrude Peckwith, August 1958

The discovery of gold in California in 1849 sparked a raging fever in thousands of Argonauts hoping to strike it rich. Among the flood of fathers, sons, brothers, and husbands that ventured west were mothers, daughters, sisters, and wives.

Pioneer women fought their way into the male-dominated field of prospecting, exposing themselves to inclement weather, rugged terrain, hostile natives, renegades, and thieves. With an influx of adventurers and rugged characters from far and near, crime was inevitable, and lady miners were as susceptible to illegal activities as everyone else.

Many prospectors were victims of raids on their camps, theft of their provisions, and claim jumping. Due to the lack of law enforcement in isolated mining towns, camp founders devised a set of protective rules to help establish some order. The "code of conduct" drafted by miners in Gold Hill, Nevada, in 1854 was direct and straight to the point:

Section 1: Any person who shall willfully and with malice aforethought take the life of any person shall upon being duly convicted thereof suffer the penalty of death by hanging.

Section 2: Any person who shall willfully wound another shall, upon conviction thereof, suffer such penalty as the jury may designate.

Section 3: Any person found guilty of robbery or theft shall, upon conviction thereof, be punished with stripes or banishment as the jury may determine.

Section 4: Any person found guilty of assault and battery, or exhibiting deadly weapons, shall upon conviction, be fined or banished as the jury may determine.

Section 5: No banking game under any consideration shall be allowed in this district, under the penalty of final banishment from the district.

Many inhabitants in and around the mining towns followed a similar set of decrees, but a contingency of bandits and bad guys thumbed their noses at the mere idea of regulating their behavior. Mrs. Julia Davis of Downieville, California, was fully aware of the criminal element that surrounded prosperous mines like the one she owned. It was their presence that prompted her to carry a pistol at all times. "No one is going to take what I worked hard to get," she told the *Sierra Citizen* newspaper in June 1911. "Anyone comes near my claim hoping this woman is going to be an easy mark, or be scared off her property, is in for a surprise."

Camps in the vicinity of Mrs. Davis were repeatedly stolen from or vandalized. Her claim, however, was left unscathed. On February 10, 1912, after more than three years of protecting her mine from swindlers and crooks, she finally struck it big. According to the *Downieville Democrat,* her property contained "some of the largest chunks of gold in the area. . . . Mrs. Davis found a piece of gold in her diggings in what is known as the Warden Ravine, about four miles above Downieville on the North Fork, Saturday morning. The specimen was solid gold, four inches long, two inches wide and nearly one inch thick. When put on the scales at John Costa Company's store, it weighed seven pounds."

Miners invaded the yellow-oak studded foothills around Downieville in 1848. The richest diggings were found near the sand bars along the Yuba River. During its heyday from 1848 to 1902, prospectors pulled more than a billion dollars worth of gold out of the mountains and streams. By the early 1900s, the gold had played out and Downieville's population dwindled from five thousand to just below twenty-two hundred people. Mining continued to be a popular career in the town, and prospectors who owned wealthy claims continued to be preyed upon by greedy malcontents.

Mine owner Gertrude Peckwith and her husband Tony worked their profitable Downieville find for years, always safeguarding that their claim was secure. In 1958, a series of unfortunate events led to Gertrude losing her tie to the mine—events that law enforcement officials and local newspaper reporters insisted were suspicious and premeditated by someone who desperately wanted the Peckwith riches.

Era Gertrude Chinn was born on June 20, 1876, in Beaver Dam, Kentucky and came to California in 1906. She was the owner and operator of a successful beauty shop in San Francisco. She met Tony Peckwith when he made a trip to the bayside city to purchase mining equipment. The two were married in 1923 and resided in Downieville for more than thirty-five years.

Gold miner Gertrude Peckwith worked the hills and streams in and around Downieville, California, in 1923. This 1852 illustration offers a view of the town's main street. The Yuba River runs alongside the gold rush camp.

Tony was an accomplished miner and a partner in a lucrative mining venture. His natural ability to locate gold made him a valuable asset to the West Point Mining Company. The rocks he discovered on the site made the local newspapers seventeen years before he and Gertrude were wed. According to the August 11, 1906 edition of the *Mountain Messenger,* "Tony Peckwith, one of the boys of the West Point Mine at Monte Cristo, exhibited some fine nuggets last Sunday, recently taken out of the above named mine. There were three of them valued at about $90 each and one nugget was about $500."

Tony invested his share of the profits made from the West Point Mine to purchase the Golden Empire Mine. He and Gertrude were the sole stockholders in the expedition; both shared the duties of digging and panning the rocks and streams in the area, and Gertrude maintained the books for the business. The couple had no children and were devoted to one another and their work. The property proved to be a worthy investment, yielding more than a quarter of a million after only a year in operation.

In 1937, Tony was killed in a mining accident at the West Point Mine. The following year Gertrude married Tony's brother, William. William also worked at the mine and in 1941, he too died in a similar accident. The widow Peckwith was left to operate the Golden Empire Mine on her own. Rumors abound that the deaths of both her husbands were planned "accidents." Unknown persons, hoping to acquire Gertrude and Tony's claim, were reported to have been behind the passing of the Peckwith brothers. Gertrude dismissed the idea outright, and despite warnings from well-meaning friends and neighbors, she refused to take precautions with her own life.

In addition to prospecting, for many years Gertrude operated a water service company. The service assisted mine owners in the area with pumping water out of their diggings. While manning the office on a warm day in the summer of 1956, she met a fifty-eight-year-old miner by the name of August Pelletier, who was working his way across the Sierra mountain range searching for gold. He believed the hills around Downieville contained a major gold vein that had not yet been tapped. His enthusiasm and excitement for the fortune was infectious and Gertrude invited him to search for the treasure in her mine.

Old timers living in town had shared information with the charming August about which mines had made money and Gertrude's Gold Eagle was one of them. Without hesitation, August quickly accepted the lady miner's offer. In a very short time the two became good friends. It is not clear if Gertrude developed romantic feelings for August, but she did care and trust him enough to give him power of attorney over her business dealings.

Downieville residents were suspicious of August's relationship with the eighty-one-year-old woman. With nothing more to go on than a gut instinct or mutual distrust of the ambitious miner, some people approached Gertrude with their feelings. She did not share their concerns and avoided anyone who made disparaging remarks about August.

On August 28, 1958, news that Mrs. Peckwith had died filtered through the area, and many townspeople believed foul play might have been involved. The *Sierra County Newspaper* carried her obituary, explaining that her passing was a result of a serious fall.

> Mrs. Era Gertrude Peckwith died about 5 o'clock this afternoon at her home. According to reports, she was traveling past the Bank Mine, on Downie River, above the Hansen bridge, formerly owned and operated by the late "Frendy" Jean Renier, which in former days had been a good prospector.
>
> She accompanied August Pelletier to the Golden Eagle Mine Wednesday morning, and according to Philip R. Newberg, coroner, Pelletier said he was working in the tunnel and came out about 11 a.m., heard her moaning and found she had fallen 30 feet over a bank toward the river. He took her home and called Dr. Carl C. Sutton who advised hospitalization, particularly on account of a heavy cold, but she declined for lack of finances. . . . Pneumonia is said to have attributed to her death. Bergemann Funeral Service came for the body and Newberg ordered an autopsy to determine cause of death.

The report that Gertrude's funds were depleted to the point that she could not afford a stay in the hospital shocked and saddened the community. Many surmised that her money had been slowly siphoned away. The autopsy report noted that Gertrude's death was indeed a result of a "fall from the trail down a steep bank while walking along a narrow trail." Investigators further concluded that the fall had been an accident.

Regardless of what the official document read, how she died was a source of continual gossip. Stories circulated that she had been drugged and that had caused her to fall. Others claim she was hit in the back of the head with a rock and that caused her to lose her footing. Copies of the autopsy report that were snuck out of the coroner's office made their way through the community and fueled the skeptics' scenario that Gertrude had been hit. According to Newberg's findings, "When the skull was open during the standard procedure, it was seen there was a large hemotoma under the scalp in the middle portion of the skull." Newberg insisted the bruise was consistent with an injury from a fall, but doubters would not be satisfied.

Conspiracy theorists even dissected the statement of eyewitness Leta Ketcham. The sixty-one-year-old woman informed investigators of everything she had seen the morning Gertrude died, beginning with the fact that her home was located across the Downie River from the Golden Eagle Mine.

I can see the Golden Eagle Mine and trail to it from my kitchen window. I have seen Mr. Pelletier and Mrs. Peckwith going to the mine by the trail many times. It was customary for Mrs. Peckwith to be walking alone along the trail in going to the mine and again in returning along the trail to the car after they were through working at the mine. I had seen Mrs. Peckwith walking along the narrow trail a number of times by herself and Mr. Pelletier would follow in about five minutes.

On August 27, 1958, about eleven o'clock, I looked out my kitchen window and saw Mrs. Peckwith hanging on to the roots of several trees near the top of the bank at the edge of the trail. Mr. Pelletier was trying to push her up on to the trail. Mr. Pelletier finally got Mrs. Peckwith on to the trail. He let her rest a few minutes and then helped her up and they started to walk along the trail. They went behind some trees and I saw them again about fifty yards down the stream. Mr. Pelletier picked Mrs. Peckwith up and carried her to the car. Mr. Pelletier then went back along the trail and got his tools and returned to the car.

I had worried many times that Mrs. Peckwith would fall from the trail as it was very narrow in spots along the banks. At times she would hang on to the brush and even crawl on her hands and knees to make her way along the trail.

Those who believed Gertrude's death was not an accident supported their premise with Ketcham's statement that she saw August and Gertrude as they "went behind some trees." Speculation rose that in that moment the lady miner could have been "knocked in the skull with a good size rock."

Throughout the ordeal and the days and weeks after Gertrude's demise, Pelletier steadfastly maintained his innocence. He vigorously denied having anything to do with her fall or with taking her money. The power of attorney she had signed over to him was terminated at her death. Gertrude's niece was named as heir of her estate and of the Golden Eagle Mine. August left Downieville for whereabouts unknown.

Gertrude's mine proved to be played out. Her relatives decided to leave the property alone and allow time and nature to reclaim the diggings.

FRANCES WILLIAMS:
FOUNDER OF THE
COALDALE MINING COMPANY

"She came, she saw, and she paid."

> —The *Goldfield Chronicle*'s comment about
> Frances's unfortunate experience
> with the Royal Flush Mine, June 1908

An early morning sun burst through the half-opened door of the assay office in the gold rush town of Tonopah, Nevada in 1903. Dr. Frances Williams, a distinguished-looking woman in her late fifties, studied a large wall map of the various mining claims in the vicinity and traced a section of road with the index finger of her gloved hand. She was dressed in fashionable garments, including a black felt hat from under which soft curls of gray peaked out.

After a few moments she turned away from the map to look at a short, squat district mining recorder reviewing a stack of papers in front of him. Although he wore heavy-lensed glasses, the paperwork was pressed to his nose as he read. Dr. Williams approached the far-sighted man and gave a slight cough. "Everything is in order," he said without looking up. "Your claim has been recorded." Frances thanked him for his time and after the clerk stamped and dated the

DR. FRANCES E. WILLIAMS.

Dr. Frances E. Williams was a fiercely independent miner who dreamed of more than finding gold—she wanted to establish a city.

document, he handed the material back to her. She tucked the paper into her woolen satchel and marched proudly out of the office.

It was a full day's trip to her property in the White Mountains, 40 miles west of Tonopah. After six long months living in a tent in the up-and-coming mining camp of Goldfield, Nevada and shifting through the gold rocks at the base of Malapai Mesa, Dr. Williams had finally secured a plot of land that promised to yield a fortune. The fifty-nine-year-old woman's 1,280 acres possessed gold and coal and an ample water supply for farmers and town sites in the lowland areas. Within five years she calculated she could become one of the wealthiest people in Nevada.

Frances Estelle Williams was born in 1844 in New England and was raised by an invalid mother for whom she assumed the responsibility of caring at a very young age. The self-sufficient, compassionate girl grew up quickly. Given her level of maturity, she was attracted to older men who she said had "personal accountability and dedication to a task." Before she was out of her teens she had married a decorated Navy surgeon, who died of heart failure shortly after they were wed.

Frances's second husband was a successful St. Louis manufacturer of shellacs, which were primarily for use on silk hats, and varnishes. The wealthy entrepreneur was forty years old and Frances was twenty. The couple was anxious to start a family and during their thirty-five years of marriage they would bring sixteen children into the world; only two children survived to adulthood. Heartbreak and an overwhelming desire to help other mothers who had struggled with the death of a baby would later prompt Frances to study medicine.

In hopes of further developing their profitable business, the Williams moved to the east coast and opened an office in New

York. Frances's husband and son, James, worked side by side creating new recipes to enhance the strength of shellac, and they grew the family-owned and -operated company into a million-dollar organization. Owing to some unwise investments, a slowing of the market, and a lack of focus, the corporation began losing funds as quickly as they were acquired. Using her natural financial talent and ability to take charge of a difficult circumstance, Frances took over the day-to-day operation of the company. She reviewed the books, managed all incoming and outgoing money, and became superintendent of the laboratory. After a few years, the fortune the Williams lost was restored.

With the shellacking and varnishing company making money again, Frances decided to pursue a degree in medicine. Her husband was not opposed to his wife's ambition; he had plans of his own to focus on. He wanted to retire from the corporate world, sell off the business, and move to Florida to become an orchard farmer. According to an article about his venture to the southeast that ran in the Tonopah, Nevada newspaper the *Pueblo Chieftan,* all did not go well: " . . . Fate seemed adverse to Mr. Williams living a life of ease. Jack Frost took a hand in the game and where at night the work of a lifetime was represented by acres of thrifty trees loaded with fruit and promises of more, in the morning naught but blackened wood and blasted hopes remained."

In 1884, Frances was again put in a position where she had to salvage the family funds and infuse capital into their bleeding bank account. At forty years of age and with her sights on becoming a physician, she moved to Boston and specialized in electric medicine. After graduation she opened her own practice and not only treated patients using the controversial method of touching an electrically charged scalpel to nerves of an infected area of the body, but also created a variety of conductor-style instruments to assist in her work.

The cold, damp New England weather had an adverse effect on the health of Frances's husband, who had moved to Boston to be with his wife when the orchard failed in Florida. In early 1901, Frances persuaded him to consider moving to a drier climate in the west. He agreed and Dr. Williams closed her busy Boston practice and headed to San Francisco, California with her spouse. She opened an office in her new location and in time, the west coast practice proved to be just as successful as the one on the east coast.

The scenic seaport town was heavily populated with gold and silver miners. Residents in the area could not help but overhear or be pulled into a conversation about major strikes or where the next lucrative claims could be found. Frances was extremely interested in such news and the notion of making a rich discovery lured her away from medicine and into the mining fields. The first mine she invested in was the Alpha Mine at Angel's Camp east of San Francisco. While working her claim there she learned about a gold ore find in Nevada near the boomtown of Tonopah.

Frances arrived in Nevada in the spring of 1903 and was the first woman in the tiny camp known as Goldfield. According to the April 23, 1905, edition of the Tonopah *Pueblo Chieftan* newspaper, "Dr. Williams braved the wilds of the desert, living in one of only six tents at the site. She invested the savings of years first in acquiring and then in defending property rights against the machinations and intrigues of trusted employees. Her actions indicate a determination in accomplishing a long cherished object, philanthropic in character, seldom found outside fiction or romance."

She was fifty-nine years old when she began her ambitious mining venture at the base of the Malapai Mountains. Frances searched the jagged cliffs and rocks for yellow nuggets like a seasoned prospector and was among the noted leaders of the camp who helped organize the Goldfield mining district.

On October 29, 1903, she filed a claim on an area of land called The Valley View. It yielded thousands of dollars worth of gold and silver and enabled her to develop claims she made in neighboring mountain ranges. Later, she established the St. Frances Gold Mining Company, which consisted of the numerous claims she had worked. The formation of the organization helped her to utilize the Goldfield interests to their fullest, attracting investors statewide.

Frances made frequent trips to Tonopah and Reno to solicit backers for her growing concerns. It was during one of those business trips that she overheard a pair of railroad executives discussing plans to purchase a stretch of land in the southern corner of the territory at a stage-stop known as Coaldale. The area was appealing for its coal deposits. If the railroad owned the land they would have a ready supply of fuel at their disposal. Coal had been discovered there in the fall of 1901 by William Groezenger, but its true value was not realized at the time. Mining and shipping the product off-site was cost prohibitive, and Groezenger abandoned the claim. The railroad officials alone knew the potential of the property and believed they had ample time to purchase an option.

The astute Dr. Williams acted quickly on the valuable information she discovered. She hurried to the location and inspected the area of land she had heard about, and working with William Groezenger, she staked a 1,280-acre claim and beat the railroad executives in securing an option on the plot. Once ownership of the coal was set, the mining entrepreneur established a town site and water rights. The Tonopah newspaper the *Pueblo Chieftan* explained the value of Frances's ingenuity in an article that ran on April 23rd, 1905:

The efforts of miner Dr. Frances Williams helped the town of Goldfield, Nevada, grow from a handful of people to more than three thousand residents by 1907. Many residents attended public drilling contests when they were held.

To enter desert land water was necessary. Away up in the White Mountains twenty miles from the coal deposits nature had cunningly hid away a stream of pure mountain water by dropping it into the earth at the head of a canon known as 'dry canon,' where but apparently few white men had ever been. This water right of 1,000 miners' inches, sufficient to irrigate twenty thousand acres of land, Dr. Williams secured and recorded.

Another area newspaper, the *Tonopah Miner,* called Frances's potentially lucrative business venture "a sensational feat." Investors she approached in New York, Boston, and California were eager to provide the money needed to build up the promising section of the state. For many years Frances had dreamed of owning several hundred acres of land and transforming the property into a city.

Her idea was to populate the newly formed town with laborers and business owners who "could and MUST own his own home and have a voice in the management of the business which furnishes him a livelihood."

According to the *Pueblo Chieftan,* Dr. Williams's plan was fully explained in the business prospectus she presented to investors. Of the 1,280 acres available for development, 320 were to be set aside strictly for mining coal and 960 acres were to be used for town site purchases. "Dr. Williams has valuable options upon developed coal lands which can be made income producing at once. Only one of the six quarter sections constituting the town site has been plotted as yet, but this has been laid out with a view to the development of a model city, additions to which can be made at any time."

Stock in the mining company Dr. Williams and William Groez-enger established was advertised for sale in newspapers from St. Louis to Boston. The initial $11 million in capital she raised came from a variety of investors. They were listed in the *Tonopah Bonanza* and referred to as "affiliated corporations. The Coaldale Mining Company invests $5 million; the Nevada Electric Power and Trans-mission Company, $5 million; and the St. Frances Mining and Smelt-ing Company, $1 million."

The prospectus—authored by Frances—offered "buy-in" opportunity for under $1,000. "To every person investing $500 in the development of these enterprises," the proposal read, "whether becoming a resident of Coaldale or not, a lot not exceeding one-fourth of an acre in the town site together with two thousand shares of the stock of the Coal Mining Company, two thousand shares of the Electric Power Company stock, and two hundred shares of the Smelting Company's stock will be given." Frances promised investors that they would receive a full quarter-acre parcel in Coaldale and see a return on their investment within the first six months. She also offered "life employment to skilled artisans in any department."

Many community leaders in Tonopah and surrounding areas objected to Frances's aggressive fund-raising campaign and warned potential investors to be careful. William Booth, editor of the *Tonopah Bonanza* newspaper, felt Frances was overconfident of success and was promising too much for an untried area. Criticism of her business methods could have easily been ignored if the plan had unfolded the way she had hoped, but when the geologist hired to test the coal informed the stockholders that the black rock would not reach its fuel grade level use for a million years, Frances was branded a charlatan.

William Booth wrote a harsh column that further called into question Frances's honesty. She sued the paper and its editor for libel and offered her side of the Coaldale events in an article in the *Tonopah Miner*. She admitted that she was guilty of certain "trifling errors," but argued against the notion that the investment was a complete bust for stockholders. Although the coal find was a disappointment, the rich soil did contain gold and the ample water supply was a moneymaker as well. She reported that the Affiliated Corporations were listed in Dun and Bradstreet (a leading provider of business information) and boasted an income of $3 million a year.

Frances vigorously defended herself to anyone who challenged her in print or in person. As if to emphasize how offended she was by the accusation that she was less than honest, she began carrying a gun. She was provoked to brandish the weapon on one occasion that involved an attorney. The local authorities were called to intervene in the still unknown dispute. Frances was arrested and later released; the attorney moved to California.

In spite of the setback, Frances continued her mining pursuits. She divided her time between prospecting, caring for her now

Main Street of Goldfield as it looked a year after Frances Williams made her initial discovery in October 1903.

invalid husband, and maintaining a small medical practice in San Francisco. In 1906, she sold her Goldfield mining claims and used the proceeds from the sale to buy an interest in the Mohawk Mine, a major gold mine in Esmeralda County, Nevada.

Frances took on mine promoter, David Mackenzie, as her partner and the two formed a corporation called the Frances-Mohawk Mining and Leasing Company. They successfully solicited investors and immediately poured the money into developing the mine. By January 1907, the mine had yielded more than $2 million for its owners and made Frances the richest female miner in the territory.

In January 1908, Frances's husband passed away. She returned to the mine fields of Nevada, but stayed only a short time before moving on to Death Valley. The gold strike had extended to the desert area and Frances had hoped to add another major discovery to her mining career. Now in her late sixties, the boisterous prospector journeyed through the Gold Mountain Range alone, bracing the fierce elements and hiking over treacherous precipices. She secured leases for mines near the town of Hornsilver, west of Goldfield, Nevada, organized the Frances Lime Point Mining Company, and sold blocks of stock in the venture for ten cents a share. Once again her shrewd assessment of a good mine paid off: For several weeks wagonloads of gold ore were removed from the location.

While Frances was overseeing the work at the Lime Point Mining Company she received word that another of her investments was about to make good. The Royal Flush claims that she had acquired during a visit through the Gold Mountains were reportedly "alive with gold." She hurried back to the area, collected samples of rock from a ledge where the find originated and waited for the assayer's office in Tonopah to provide her with the results. It was gold.

After establishing yet another corporation, this one called the Frances Gold Mountain Mining Company, she began selling stock in the business. The motive many of the financial backers had to invest in the company was that they believed Frances's mine was really the Lost Breyfogle Ledge. Legend had it that a prospector named Charles Breyfogle found the rich outcropping in 1860, but when he stepped out of the mountains and into Death Valley, he became disoriented with thirst and heat. As a result he couldn't recall the exact location of the find. Frances encouraged the idea that her claim was the same one Breyfogle had discovered and it produced the desired effect, increasing the sale of stock in the company and generating more revenue for mining operations.

Throughout the winter of 1908 and into the spring of 1909, Frances managed the business at the Royal Flush and Lime Point mines. With the exception of an encouraging amount of gold ore gleaned at the onset of the dig, neither mine did as well as Frances anticipated. Bank failures that hit institutions across the United States took their toll on the company's funds and a lawsuit filed against the Frances-Mohawk Mine by a rival mining company for improper timbering placed the doctor's shrinking income further away. Attempts by Frances's lawyers to settle the lawsuit to avoid going to court were unsuccessful. The trial began in late March 1909 at the Goldfield Courthouse. The strain of the legal proceedings and near financial ruin left Frances despondent and tired.

On March 24, 1909, Frances suffered a massive heart attack and died. Fellow Goldfield pioneer Richard L. Colburn remembered Dr. Williams as "the most lovable woman that it has ever been my pleasure to meet." Frances's only living son, James, assumed control of his mother's claims.

LILLIAN MALCOLM:
PROSPECTOR IN THE
SILVER PEAK MOUNTAINS

"The grandest and healthiest life known is this rough pioneer life. And I don't see why more women are not in the hills."

—Lillian Malcolm, 1905

A handsome wisp of a woman stepped out on the deck of the steamship *City of Seattle* and peered into the dazzling sunlight reflecting off the mountains surrounding the harbor in Dawson City, Yukon. Thirty-nine years old, Lillian Malcolm's heart contracted with excitement and a strong sense of longing as she breathed in the clean, frigid air and watched the icy cliffs looming ahead. The spectacular scenery caused a hush to fall over the travelers aboard the ship and in the quiet the shifting, grinding, and settling of the glaciers could be heard.

As a stage actress who had recently performed in New York opposite the noted Shakespearian actor Frederick Warde, Lillian was accustomed to traveling to distant locales with impressive settings. The Yukon's stark white views and crystal-clear waters provided her with a sight that paled in comparison to any other she had ever seen. She was confident her travels into what she referred

Trailblazer Lillian Malcolm filed claims on gold mines from Alaska to Nevada, unearthing a fortune in the process.

to as the "wild and beautiful territory" would be the adventure she had always longed for.

In 1898, Lillian followed gold stampeders to the spot at the confluence of the Yukon and Klondike rivers in search of a multitude of riches. Upon her arrival she purchased a generous amount of mining supplies, food, and warm clothing, loaded the inventory onto a dogsled, and mushed her team into the range of broken, snowy peaks in the distance. Driven by a fever to find a fortune, Lillian made her way along the Chilkoot Trail, a thirty-mile journey climbing 3,500 feet.

Born in 1868 in the northeast to wealthy parents of Scottish descent, Lillian Katheryn Malcolm's initial ambition was to become an actress. Given that women involved in that profession in 1880 were considered to have questionable morals, the Malcolms had reservations about their daughter's intended line of work. Lillian was not swayed by disapproving attitudes; indeed, she thrived on pursuing nontraditional ways for women to make a living.

Entering the field of prospecting raised the eyebrows of the so-called proper ladies in the more civilized areas of the Yukon region. "I would notice, as I passed down the street of a mining camp, clad in my tallow-spattered Khakis," Lillian relayed in an article for the *Nevada Humboldt Star* newspaper in 1905, "the wives of struggling clerks and other low-salaried men held their garments aside as though I might contaminate them."

In addition to criticism from her own sex about her choice of employment, Lillian suffered through freezing temperatures and a rugged terrain on her way to stake out claims in Kugarak and Nome, Alaska. Her gold findings were minimal, but it was enough to spur her on to the next mine or riverbed suspected of being rich. The trek across the frozen landscape was fraught with risks. While making her way along the Bering Sea near the Gulf of Alaska in 1899, Lillian encountered fast-melting glaciers that forced her to jump from iceberg to iceberg drifting on the water.

By 1900, the actress-turned-prospector had taken up residence in a lodging house in a small mining camp in Nome. During the day she vigorously searched for gold and at the end of the long work period, she regaled other sourdoughs with tales of her northwest gold rush experiences. On numerous occasions saloon keepers and dance hall owners tried to persuade her to abandon her mining pursuits and work for them as an entertainer. Owing to the persistence of her nature and complete confidence that she would locate a rich strike, she refused.

Claim jumpers were a serious problem for miners who had staked out a section of land and were diligently working the spot. Lillian was not exempt from the land grabbers' violent attempts to roust miners off their property. Although she carried a gun and knew how to use it, it was not enough to keep thieves from overtaking her land and driving her away. The court system in the remote areas of Alaska was corrupt and judges were given bribes to side with the criminals. In spite of her steadfast efforts, the mining claims Lillian filed remained in question and she was unable to get the property back. After more than a year of trying to overturn the matter, she abandoned the pursuit and returned to the States.

News of a silver strike in Tonopah prompted Lillian to relocate to the boomtown. With very little money and only a few changes of clothes, she managed to convince a business owner to let her stay at one of their hotels. In exchange for room and board, Lillian agreed to entertain residents with stories of her theatrical career and mining adventures. The occasional odd job helped her to earn the funds needed to invest in mining supplies and a burro. She prospected in the hills around Tonopah and nearby Goldfield, and in 1903 she worked a small section of land in the Silver Peak mountain range. The property did not yield the income she'd hoped for and by 1905 she was on the move again.

Following yet another cry of gold, Lillian hurried to a thriving mining community called Rhyolite not far from Death Valley. More than two thousand claims spanning a thirty-mile area around the town made the region attractive to Lillian. No sooner had she arrived did she agree to go into business with another miner, the founder of Rhyolite, Frank "Shorty" Harris, who possessed the same insatiable appetite for discovering major gold finds as Lillian did. He believed that the bluffs of Death Valley contained an abundance of gold and agreed to co-finance a mining expedition into the area. Lillian led the outing accompanied by three able prospectors: George Pegot, Tom McCabe, and Anthony McCauley.

Three days after setting off on the journey the explorers lost some of the pack animals carrying their provisions. A few of the burros walked off cliffs and ledges, breaking bones and their necks; others succumbed to illness and died. As a result of the misfortune, the journey had to be cut short by three months. The quartet returned to Rhyolite, but a determined Lillian quickly organized another expedition and set off again for the area where Harris suggested mining should take place.

Lillian was grateful for another chance at a possible fortune and hoped a woman's participation in such a quest would entice other females to the field. "The higher branches of mining offer great inducements to women," Lillian told a Nevada newspaper reporter before embarking on her second prospecting trip into Death Valley. "I don't mean the kind of work I am doing. But there is surveying and drafting, the study of mineralogy and geology. It is clean, honest money. There is too much hypocrisy in the sexes. Women can endure as much as a man. Comply with the law and you will have man's responsibilities and man's reward."

Shorty Harris teamed up with Lillian on the foray and the pair spent two months investigating the high desert. The talented miner later transformed the sight of spectacular wildflowers, snow-covered peaks, beautiful sand dunes, intermittent streams, and wildlife she encountered during her travels into spirited stories told to other prospectors and their families. Lillian and Harris scaled mountainsides and waded through waist-high creeks, staking out claims along the way and meeting interesting characters who made their homes in the remote location.

Walter Scott, better known as Mysterious Scott, was one such character. He was a former cowboy actor turned prospector who lived under a rock outcropping in the Black Mountains. Scott was an eccentric, charismatic man who could skillfully con people out of their gold nuggets and gold claims. Lillian was unimpressed with his manner and was suspicious of his kindness. She did, however, have more than a passing interest in his mining partner, Bill Key, a soft-spoken, easygoing, half-Indian man whom she recognized as being manipulated by Mysterious Scott. He had staked a few rich claims on his own and Scott was trying to wrangle the find away from him. Lillian befriended the gullible Key and persuaded him to allow her to take out an option on his property. The agreement promised to give him a chance to work the claims himself and get out from under Scott's control. Key agreed, and when Lillian returned to Rhyolite on January 2, 1906, she had more than her future in gold mining to think about.

With Lillian some distance from Death Valley and unable to keep Key away from Scott, the crafty miner zeroed in on his reliable but simple-minded business associate and convinced him to abandon his hunt for gold and help him kill a man. The intended victim was a mining engineer hired by east coast investors to develop the riches in the area. Scott wanted the engineer stopped and believed Key was the man for the job. For reasons that have never been revealed, the plan was thwarted.

When news of the botched crime reached Lillian along with the information that Scott was trying to frame Key for the murder attempt, she hurried to Key's side. He was being held at the San Bernardino jail and Lillian hired the best attorney in the area to defend him. The attorney managed to persuade the court to dismiss the charges. Key was grateful for Lillian's efforts, but he did not feel for her as she did for him. Upon his release he returned to his gold mine in Death Valley, and a brokenhearted Lillian moved back to Tonopah.

After relocating to the Nevada boomtown where she once lived, Lillian revisited her mines in the Silver Peak Range. As in 1903, the cluster of claims near Coyote Springs appeared to be the most promising. She needed capital to develop the area further and sought out funds from the Pittsburgh Mining Company operating near her property. Although the mining stocks and investments were at an all-time low, she managed to secure the bankroll needed to do the work.

"I raised the money in Pittsburgh," she told the *Tonopah Bonanza* in November 1907, "and I had no trouble in doing it, which goes to show that there is a great deal of bugaboo about this talk of hard times and stringency of the money market. There is plenty of money to be had for legitimate propositions, if one is sincere in his or her motives. When one goes to businessmen, all that is necessary is to talk common sense. But if one is going to take romantic flights, and go up into millions on an ordinary proposition, he is going to fall short in his expectations."

If Lillian's mining venture, aptly named The Scotch Lassie Gold Mining Company, had proved to be as profitable as she had imagined, she wanted to use her earnings to create an organization to assist destitute women. Unfortunately, the mining operation was a failure or "humbug," as miners called it. Her disappointment in the venture was short-lived and in the spring of 1907, she pressed on to yet another area rumored to possess gold.

Lillian's next stop was the Alta Mining District, south of Nogales, Mexico. She found very little gold in the region, but refused to abandon the notion that a bonanza was within her reach. By mid-1911 she was back in Nevada again working claims in Humboldt County.

Lillian was now forty-three years old and had thirteen years of mining experience under her belt. Her looks reflected the difficult line of work she had subscribed to. A reporter for the *Tonopah Bonanza* wrote that she had a "refinement that the desert could not mar." He continued in a 1907 article: "Her hair was braided and tied in numerous labor saving knots with white baby ribbon. This rather fantastic effort formed the background for a face that was once called pretty, but which has now certainly lost much of its feminine delicacy owing to the sun's rays of Death Valley."

Clad in her standard khaki pants, tan colored men's boots, and a narrow-brimmed felt hat, Lillian trekked from one end of Nevada to another combing the land for gold ore. In 1914, the state's mining prospects had all but faded away. In spite of that fact and with pick and shovel in hand, Lillian traipsed through the Jarbride Mountains in what would be her final mining tour. "I'm in the mining game to stay," she steadfastly told the *Reno Evening Gazette*.

Lillian drifted into Arizona in 1915 and nothing more was ever heard of her again. When and how she died remains a mystery. However lackluster her mining ventures turned out to be, she realized her dream of taking to the goldfields and developing her potential as a prospector.

In 1869 an elderly Argonaut posted a sign on the outside of his tent that read ALL AND EVERYBODY, THIS IS MY CLAIM, WHAT I WAS BORN TO DO. FIFTY FEET ON THE GULCH, CORDIN TO CLEAR CREEK DISTRICT LAW, BACKED UP BY SHOTGUN AMENDMENTS. Lillian Malcolm embodied the sentiment of the armed gold rush stampeders and did what she believed she was born to do.

JOSIE PEARL:
OWNER/OPERATOR
OF THE JUANITA MINE

"A girl can do anything if she makes up her mind to do it. And she can do it without help if she must—just two hands and trust in God!"

—Advice Josie received from her mother
when she was nine, June 1882

Thirteen-year-old Josie Reed hurried past the brush and trees lining a crude trail leading the way to the Sangre de Cristo Mountains outside of Tres Piedras, New Mexico. She moved with the ease of one who had a long acquaintance of the terrain, dodging boulders and logs that at times blocked the narrow footpath. A cheek-to-cheek grin dominated the young girl's angelic, chubby, round face and her blue-green eyes were wide with excitement. She stopped running only for a moment to yield the right of way to a pair of rabbits passing in front of her.

During the brief pause she inspected five broken pieces of rock held tightly in her right fist. Flecks of gold glittered in the sunlight. Her left arm, which was obviously broken, rested in a sling draped around her neck. Josie tucked the precious nuggets inside the folds of the cloth bandage tightly binding her left wrist.

Confident that her discovery was in a safe place, she dashed off again.

In the near distance she spotted her sister Liss and Liss's husband's cabin. Smoke swirled out of the chimney of the small log home, and the smell of freshly baked bread permeated the air. She was certain the news that she'd found gold would be a tremendous financial boost to her hard-working sibling, who was expecting her first child.

Josie had moved in with her to help with the housework and livestock and most of the time readily fulfilled her obligation, but there were days she could not resist sneaking off to the mountains to prospect. It was her life's ambition to become a miner. She wanted to follow in the footsteps of her father and brother-in-law. Both were employed at coal mines in the area but had no experience mining gold, silver, or copper.

Before her stay with Liss, Josie lived with her father. He was a great encourager of her dreams and occasionally allowed her to shadow him on his mining job. One winter day while she was off working her own diggings in the bluffs around Tres Piedras, she fell on a patch of ice and broke the bones in her forearm.

Josie's father could not look after her and work at the same time and Liss needed help, so the decision was made that she should go and live with her sister. Josie was sad about the arrangement at first, but the daily treks into the wilderness to Rat Creek and back again to look for firewood gave her the chance to continue prospecting. Her attitude improved in light of the opportunity and she grew to appreciate the setting. "If I hadn't been looking for timber," Josie admitted to thinking years later, "I never would have found gold."

Josie's discovery in late 1886 was met with great enthusiasm, and her father escorted her to the nearest assayer's office to authenticate

Josie Pearl worked her gold and silver mines in Nevada until her death at the age of 89.

the find. The nuggets proved to be real gold and a claim on the spot where the rocks had been located was filed. Josie named her mine the Molly S. Within a few days of the filing, the teenager was offered $5,000 for the Molly S. and she accepted. She used the money to pay the taxes on the family farm, add another room onto the Reed home, purchase feed for the animals, shoes, and bolts of fabric for clothes to be made for her brothers and sisters. Josie vowed then that as long as she lived she would hunt for gold.

Josephine Reed was born on December 19, 1873, in Evening Shade, Arkansas. The prospecting phenomenon was one of twelve children. Her mother, Priscilla Adair, and her father, John Everett Reed, made the trip overland in the fall of 1880. Reed was a farmer and rancher who had migrated to Colorado and settled in the San Luis Valley. Josie was nine when they arrived in central Colorado. Her father staked out a few acres of land for his family and built an adobe house on the property. "The walls were made of mud brick," Josie recalled in her autobiography. "There were no windows except the panes of glass set in the mud walls, and they could not be opened. The door consisted of cottonwood, over which burlap was stretched. This allowed circulation of air, since there was a large fireplace in the home. Thus, there was plenty of mud in the winter, and stifling heat in the summer. We dared not open the door for ventilation, or we would be pestered to death with flies."

Josie's father went to work farming, and she and her brother and sisters kept busy with school and their chores. The Reed children took odd jobs to help supplement the income for the large family. Josie was a midwife's assistant and a dishwasher at a local hotel. When she wasn't working she explored the trails around her home, looking for the gold nuggets she had heard were in abundance in various parts of the state.

The need to keep his wife and children clothed and fed prompted John Reed to pursue employment as a coal miner in New Mexico. Farming did not supply a steady income and he believed mining would. He left his sons to tend to the crops and made plans to leave the area as soon as possible. Josie had accompanied John on previous trips to Tres Piedras and was fascinated with mining, the machinery, and the tools; she wanted to join her father on this venture. After several requests, Josie's parents agreed that she could leave with John.

Father and daughter lived in one of the many shacks clustered around the mine. Josie kept house during the day, and in the evenings and weekends she and John would visit with the other miners on the site. One of the laborers taught Josie how to pan for gold and how to tell the difference between iron pyrite or crystal quartz.

The sale of the Molly S. mine enabled John to return to the family farm in Colorado to visit. Josie went home for a few months, but it was clear to her that she couldn't stay and needed to be on her own. Like her older sister before her, she moved to Denver to attend Peck's Training School. Her education consisted of classes in cooking, sewing, and various household duties. Josie enjoyed her time at school and was exceptional at cooking, but she grew increasingly homesick for the Sangre de Cristo Mountains and prospecting. She longed to return to the area but lacked the funds to make the trip or to finance a mining expedition.

Josie graduated from Peck's in 1888 and immediately took a job as a pastry cook at the James Hotel in Leadville. The popular business attracted many mine workers and owners including Horace Tabor and his wife, the infamous Baby Doe. The Tabors were millionaires and fans of the biscuits Josie made—she made eight hundred a day. They befriended the young girl and discussed business and mining with her whenever they came into the establishment for food. They invited Josie on sleigh rides and to several fancy area dances. Josie came to regard Horace and Baby Doe as a benevolent aunt and uncle. The Tabors were protective of the teenager and they kept a close eye on her well being. The mining district was crowded with unscrupulous men who would take advantage of a single young girl away from her parents. When Josie tired of Leadville and expressed a desire to return home, Baby Doe offered to purchase a train ticket for her.

Josie arrived back in the San Luis Valley just in time to witness a mass exodus of the area's residents west to the San Juan Mountains. Silver had been discovered and farmers traded in their plows for pickaxes and headed for the hills. Josie found that she was just as anxious as her neighbors to pursue mining. Although she was happy to be with her family again, she had become too independent to stay in the house cooking and cleaning. She wanted to prospect. An offer from the Tabors to take Josie with them to the new mining town of Creede, Colorado was quickly accepted by the restless teenager.

After agreeing to serve as the Tabor's chief cook in exchange for room and board and the opportunity to search for her own strike, Josie packed her meager belongings and moved away again. The trip from San Luis Valley to Creede was long and uncomfortable. The new mining camp was overflowing with prospectors who had rushed in to dig for silver. The region had been given the nickname "King of Solomon's Mining District" and everywhere Josie looked were men roaming in and out of makeshift saloons and gambling houses carrying picks and shovels.

"I know your mother was worried about your coming with us to this raucous and bawdy place," Baby Doe told her, "but your father insisted you could hold your own."

"I certainly can," Josie replied as they rode down the main section of Creede toward the Zang Hotel where Josie would reside for the next few months.

The Tabors introduced Josie to many of the business owners in the camp the day after they had settled in their new home. Among the popular characters living in Creede were sporting-house owner Soapy Smith; gambler Mort Watrous; Bob Ford, the man who shot Jesse James; and Army scout and sometime miner herself, Calamity Jane.

When Josie wasn't cooking for the Tabors and holding down a job in the kitchen at the Zang Hotel, she was roaming the landscape outside of town looking for silver and gold ore. Horace and Baby Doe eventually returned to Denver, leaving their protégé behind to fend for herself and to keep an eye on their claim, the Amethyst Mine. By January 1893, two years after the Tabors had brought Josie to town, she still had not been able to locate a substantial find of her own. She was frustrated and tired of the "rowdy, drunken sots" she encountered everyday. "I wish a real man would come to town," she lamented to one of her friends.

The Silver Act Amendment of November 1, 1893, which regulated the value of silver, sending the price for the metal spiraling downward and making it no longer profitable to mine, forced some of the mines to close and drove numerous miners out of town. However, Government-funded engineers were moving into Creede to oversee the removal of the silver ore for use in making coins. Josie had the good fortune to make the acquaintance of one of those mining engineers while dining with a friend. Lane Pearl was a graduate of Leland Stanford University and had relocated to the area. He was six feet fall and handsome. He had an engaging personality and a pleasant, soft-spoken voice.

Josie and Lane were instantly smitten with one another and spent a great deal of time together. They were married in late 1903 at the Reed family farm. After the wedding the couple returned to Creede and purchased a home near the Happy Thought Mine where Lane was foreman. Josie loved her new husband but knew she would not be content as a full-time housewife; she liked working in between prospecting ventures. With Lane's full support she accepted a position in town as the manager of a miner's boardinghouse. That job led to an offer to manage a hospital in a mining camp five miles above Creede.

Although she excelled at her work, nothing she did compared to prospecting. "It was all I dreamed about," she wrote in her autobiography. "If I could just find a good prospect! With Lane a mining engineer, we could develop a mine by doing the initial work ourselves and then hiring men and installing machinery as conditions warranted." Josie was convinced that she would find what she was looking for. Lane called her persistent search "mining fever."

As the director of the Bachelor Hospital, Josie was on call twenty-four hours a day, seven days a week and worked almost exclusively with miners. She oversaw the treatment of prospectors injured in work-related accidents or suffering from the inhalation of silica dust from the mines. The hours were grueling and the job cut drastically into the time she needed to look for gold and silver. She decided to resign her position and take a less stressful job at the Last Chance Mine Boardinghouse. Her new post gave her the opportunity to try and locate a rich mine of her own. Prospecting in the high peaks and rocky gulches, Josie survived numerous avalanches and startling encounters with bears and mountain lions living in the timber. There was no danger she was not willing to endure to find the mother lode.

Miners from Bachelor, Leadville, and Cripple Creek who stayed at the Last Chance boardinghouse benefited from Josie's knowledge of prospecting and kindness. Men who had profitable claims rewarded her for her good cooking and mining tips with $100 bills and gold earrings. She never let a down-on-his-luck miner leave her establishment hungry and she always defended foreign workers brought in to replace miners on strike from various mining companies. The foreign miners who sorted ore were mistreated frequently; they were beaten, tied to trees, and left to die of exposure. With Lane's support, Josie rescued several of the men from certain death. Her own life was threatened on more than a few occasions for interfering with what the so-called "honest miners" insisted they do.

The Pearls returned to Creede in 1905 where Lane took a job as shift boss for the Capta Vinta Mine. The couple moved into a small cabin near the mine and while Lane was off at work, Josie prospected. One day while she was out pounding some ore in an iron mortar she noticed a red glow coming from the Capta Vinta Mine. The mine was on fire and Lane and his men were trapped inside. Josie helped organize a rescue crew to subdue the flames and pull the miners out of the burning shaft. The men were blistered and suffering from smoke inhalation, but all survived.

The near death experience prompted the Pearls to head back to San Luis Valley. Lane accepted a job at the Pass-Me-By Mine, sixty-five miles from Monte Vista. After building a combination home and boardinghouse, Josie negotiated a deal with the mine owner to hire her to feed and house the miners in their employ. She served fifty men three meals a day at a cost of $35 a month for food and quarters.

Josie was earning a substantial monthly income as a cook, but her desire to make the same amount by mining never wavered. In

1906, Lane and Josie leased a silver mine called the Commodore. Josie worked the mine in between serving meals at the boarding-house. The decrease in the value of silver, however, forced the pair to eventually give up the lease and accept a $40,000 loss. The decision to surrender the lease was heartbreaking for Josie, but she stubbornly held onto the notion of finding another rich strike somewhere.

The determined prospector and her husband were on the move again in 1908. News of the rich ore deposits being mined in the area around Goldfield, Colorado prompted the couple to try their luck at that location. Lane's background in mine engineering made him a highly sought-after employee. Josie's managerial skills landed her a job at the Palm Restaurant, where much of the gold dug out of the earth passed through her hands.

On her days off Josie trekked into the mountains to search for gold and silver. She would saddle her horse, loading the animal down with food, water, blankets, picks, shovels, and gold pans, and rode toward the regions of Summit King and the Bullfrog. "I always felt closer to God when I was in the mountains," she admitted in her autobiography. "The solitude was good for my soul! I often stayed overnight in the mountains and returned in the morning just in time to dress for work."

The Pearls' stay in Goldfield was short-lived. When Lane was offered the position of manager of the Ward Mine in Ely, Nevada, the two moved again. Gold had been discovered in Ely in 1900 and the town quickly became a booming mining camp. Josie cooked for the employees of Ward Mine while Lane handled the daily operation of the claim. Continually lured by the quest for gold, Josie resumed her prospecting ventures. Finally, her relentless searching paid off. She located three gold claims and named them the Nevada, the Colorado, and the Mexico.

In the midst of Josie's good fortune came the news that her friend Baby Doe Tabor had fallen on hard times, both financially and physically. She quickly made her way to Leadville to see how she could be of help. Horace had died in 1899 and Baby Doe was sick with the flu. Josie stayed by the woman's side until she became well again and then returned to Nevada.

Safely back in Ely, Josie worked her mines, supplementing her income with a job managing the Steptoe Hotel. She befriended many residents, monetarily assisted destitute miners and retired schoolteachers, held a variety of civic leadership roles, and in 1917, helped introduce and pass a bill in the Nevada State Legislature revising the pension law for retired schoolteachers.

In 1918, after more than fifteen years of marriage, Josie lost her beloved Lane when he died of influenza. She sank into a deep depression and for a time believed there was no reason to keep living. A need greater than her own heartache helped her to find a way through the sorrow. A massive snowstorm had blocked the roads leading to the mountain where the Ward Mine was located, and consequently necessary supplies for the mine and its staff were delayed. Josie offered to drive a team of horses to Ely to retrieve the provisions. The mine's temporary manager tried to talk Josie out of making the trip, but it was to no avail. "You need supplies and mail!" she told him. "One only dies once, and now I haven't much to live for, so I'll try it." The trip was rugged, but Josie made it through and returned to the Ward Mine with food, mining equipment, and other provisions intact.

Josie decided to leave the area in the spring of 1919 and travel to Los Angeles, California. She spent a great deal of time alone, walking along the beaches, still grieving the loss of Lane. After months of soul searching she made her way back to her parents' home in Colorado. It was during her brief visit that her love for mining resurfaced. She chased silver and gold strikes to Tonopah and Searchlight in Clark County, Nevada, and to Bodie and Humboldt County, California.

By the fall of 1920 Josie had settled near the town of Battle Mountain, Nevada and was employed as a cook at a boardinghouse. Her desire to devote her entire life to mining, filing claims, developing and digging shafts, and tunneling into Battle Mountain itself never wavered. As always her job cooking for miners, now at the Big Enough Mine, gave her the funds needed to keep working towards her ultimate goal.

Once she raised enough money for another mining expedition she moved on to the vicinity of Winnemucca, Nevada. She had overheard a couple of prospectors in Battle Mountain discussing the gold fields in the area between Winnemucca and a camp known as Varryville. Josie bought a burro, loaded the animal with supplies and rode off to find her fortune. She spent many days and nights alone, crushing rocks and panning them in the sands and mud of creek bottoms in the area. During her travels she met a couple of miners who had secured several rich claims in the canyons she was working. One evening she offered to make dinner for the prospectors and after tasting her delicious cooking they gave her a mine as a present. She named her claim Juanita.

The Juanita Mine proved to be rich with gold ore. Josie made enough money to not only keep herself in supplies, but she was also able to put some money in savings. In addition to the income from the Juanita, she managed to earn extra funds assisting other prospectors with their claims. While Josie was helping a handful of miners at the Opalite Mine in the spring of 1922, three men snuck onto her property and began stealing ore from the Juanita.

Josie quickly returned to her claim and discovered that the night watchman she had hired to guard the mine was part of the trio high-grading from her. The thieves plotted to kill her, but she snuck away from them during the night while they slept. She fled to a nearby miners' camp, borrowed a weapon from one of the prospectors, and snuck back to Juanita.

The following morning, armed with a rifle, she confronted the men. "Line up and keep your hands in front of you," she told them. "I don't mind shooting one little bit. In fact my trigger finger is itching to fire just in case you boys start any funny business." The men took her at her word and submitted to her demands. Cowpunchers from the nearby Montera Ranch helped escort the criminals to the authorities in Winnemucca.

Josie stayed on her own claim for the next two years, making so much money she was able to hire men to work with her and purchase new drilling equipment and ore cars. In 1929, Juanita yielded more then forty buckets of ore a day and paid out more than $15,000 a month. When the depression hit in 1930, Josie lost the entire fortune she had acquired overnight. "It's just my luck," she lamented in her biography. "Rich one day and poor the next!"

From 1930 to 1934, Josie wandered through northern California and Nevada prospecting. She filed claims on two mines in the area of Cove Canyon, Nevada. Both finds were rich with gold ore and by the end of 1936, she had made another fortune. She used her wealth to help care for the indigent women and orphaned children in the territory and for medicine and supplies for flu victims.

In 1939, sixty-six-year-old Josie returned to the Juanita Mine to work and live out the remainder of her life. Her benevolence extended to the people in the towns, villages, and Indian reservations around Winnemucca. She purchased a cemetery in the Black

Rock Desert where homeless miners with no families and the disenfranchised could be buried. She paid for the deceased to be laid to rest in wooden coffins and have their graves marked with wooden crosses. When World War II broke out, Josie decided to sell her complete interest in the Juanita Mine and the group of mines surrounding it to assist in the war effort. She also helped sell war bonds and organized scrap metal and rubber drives.

Newspaper reporter Ernie Pyle wrote a series of articles about Josie's generosity and life as a prospector. As a result of the article radio and television producers sought Josie out to appear on various broadcasts. Although she was flattered, she graciously declined any offer to participate. "You know," Josie later admitted, "I can drive a truck and work all day in the mines along with any man, but I can't stand that kind of life! I'd be worse than a pet raccoon."

Josie died of heart disease in 1962 after a brief stay at a hospital in Reno. Her last days were spent talking about life as it had been with her husband Lane and making plans to prospect for uranium.

CHARLEY HATFIELD:
MINER AT COLORADO'S PIKES PEAK

"It was hard work. Harder than just about anything I ever did."
—Charley Hatfield's thoughts about gold mining, 1861

C harley Hatfield shook a massive wooden rocker resting in a creek bed several yards from the base of Pikes Peak in Colorado. He sloshed it from side to side in the clear mountain water, and pieces of gravel sifted through the crude screen on the device. Charley's rough hands carefully inspected the yellow rocks that remained in the miner's pan. Gold nuggets gleamed up at the miner and he smiled. Other prospectors in close proximity of the find shot angry, envious looks at his discovery. He cast a wary glance around, pocketed the gold, and returned to his work.

The need to keep a watchful eye out for greedy competitors who might jump his claim was great. Charley glanced over at his primitive camp and gear and spotted a double-barreled shotgun. Should anything go wrong he was ready to handle the situation. The two revolvers in his belt and the sheath knife in his bootleg offered him an added sense of security against predators of any kind.

Fellow prospector George West watched the potentially volatile scene from his own claim downstream from Charley's.

The tall, handsome man ran his rope-calloused hands through his brick-red hair as he surveyed Charley's camp and belongings. Once he was sure the greedy eyes of the competing miners had turned away from his friend's claim he returned to his own work. Charley was one of his best friends and would help defend him if any trouble arose; he had done so on a couple of similar occasions.

George surrendered a pan of worthless rock back to the creek and removed a half-smoked cigarette from his pocket. Searching his clothes for a match to light his smoke he came across a handwritten note scrawled across a scrap of paper, tucked into his shirt. He scanned the faces of the miners around him wondering who would have given him the note and when they did it. There wasn't anyone he considered a likely candidate.

He watched Charley step out of the stream and load a sack of gold nuggets into a saddlebag draped over a tree branch. He nodded approvingly to George. George nodded back, unfolded the note and began to read. The handwriting was neat and every line was evenly spaced.

Friend George, I cannot wait to thank you for your unselfish kindness to me, and that of your pards. I must be in Gregory Gulch by ten o'clock today or perhaps lose the opportunity of my strange life in these mountains.

I cannot wait to catch my mule, but will walk to Tucker's Gulch and get a pony from John Scott for the trip. Will you please have her stabled for me by Saturday when I will be down, and can then perhaps fulfill my promise to you of giving something of my history. Be sure you are the only man, woman, or child west of the Missouri river that will ever have it from my lips. I am dreadfully tired, but I must go to Gregory this morning. Goodbye until Saturday. Charley.

George looked up from the note hoping to see Charley before he had left the area, but the miner had already disappeared into the thick spruce trees that lined the site. George studied the note again then placed it back into his pocket. Curiosity about Charley's history left him too preoccupied to continue panning.

Within a week after receiving Charley's note, George met up with the mysterious miner at a ranch near Golden, Colorado. The secret the fearless prospector had to share was that he was a she. For fifteen years Charley had masqueraded as a man. What began as the means for a thirteen-year-old orphan girl to secure employment in 1850 grew to include a way for her to serve her country as a soldier, work as a miner, and seek revenge against the desperado who had murdered her husband.

Charley would not agree to tell George her story until he promised to keep it a secret for twenty-five years. She had built a life around the male disguise and divulging the information would affect her livelihood. George, who was the publisher of the *Colorado Transcript* newspaper as well as a part-time miner, pledged that Charley's true identity would be safe with him forever if she chose. "My name is Charlotte," she told George. "My friends call me Charley." The circumstances surrounding Charley's birth in 1837 were just as controversial as the life she would later lead.

Charlotte was the product of an affair between two lovesick people who had pledged themselves to one another for an eternity. They were eager to marry, but their nuptials were postponed by a death in the family. Charlotte's father left his betrothed in Louisiana, where they lived, to settle the estate he had inherited in Kentucky. For a while the pair continued their romance through the mail. But when the letters stopped coming, Charlotte's mother assumed the young man had had a change of heart, and she married another. When her fiancé eventually returned and learned that his beloved had wed, he was heartbroken. After a brief encounter, the two separated. He left her to her husband and returned to France where he was born. He never knew he had a daughter.

Ashamed and financially unable to care for her child, Charlotte's mother sent her to live with her uncle in New Orleans. Charlotte was raised to believe that her parents had died and that her mother was her aunt. It wasn't until Charlotte was fifteen that she learned the truth. Looking back over her childhood, she remembered how her aunt's eyes would fill up with tears and her voice would choke back sobs when they were together. She later recalled, "My remembrance of the place and its people are misty—all about it seems more like something I once saw in a dream, but whose characters time has effaced."

At the age of twelve, Charley left the boarding school where her uncle had sent her and married a riverboat pilot. She wrote that he was a "noble fellow and well repaid the sacrifice made for him." When her uncle heard about the elopement, he disowned her. She was so much in love with her husband that she dismissed her uncle's reaction outright: "I did not regret getting married. . . . I was happy beyond my most sanguine expectations," she would later recall.

By the couple's third year of marriage, they had two children, a boy and a girl. Charlotte was elated with her life. "I believe that now the circle of my enjoyment is complete. My husband, though much absent, was remitting in his love—I had two bright, healthy children, what more could a woman ask?"

Our Pack Train, Pike's Peak Trail.

Charley Hatfield traversed the hills where these prospectors stand with their burros on a trail on Pikes Peak.

Charley wouldn't know happiness for long. Three months after the birth of her daughter, news came that her husband had been killed. "A man named Jamieson . . . ." the messenger reluctantly began. "They argued over an old grudge and then Jamieson shot your husband." Charley went through the next month of her life in a fog, devastated by her loss. After paying for her husband's burial and settling his outstanding accounts, she had very little money left to support her children. Being a woman and untrained for any profession, she found acquiring reputable work impossible. She decided to disguise herself as a man to gain employment and set about to make a new life for herself.

Charley was convincing as a man. She cut her hair to the proper length and donned a suit. Her appearance did not differ materially from that of any boy of fifteen or sixteen. She found a job as a cabin boy on a steamer and rose through the ranks to eventually become a pantry man.

Once a month she would change back into her dresses and petticoats and visit her children. Her absence from them was tortuous, she later recalled in her autobiography: "My children would haunt my dreams and play about me in my waking hours—the separation seemed intolerable, and for the first month an eternity."

Charley's work would take her up and down the rivers of the Midwest. She kept a keen eye out for Jamieson at every port. Her first confrontation with Jamieson, outside Schell's Saloon, had left her with a broken thigh. It would take six months for her to heal. Once she was up and around, she decided to head for the "Land of Gold."

In the spring of 1855, she joined a wagon train as a bushwhacker and took off for California—the only woman in a party of sixty men. Charley recorded her overland route in great detail. Her diary included such trail markers as Court House, Chimney Rock,

Scotts Bluff, Mormon Ferry, and Independence Rock. Her journal would later be used to guide several wagon trains bound for California and Oregon.

The way west was full of every kind of danger and privation. Charley lost 110 head of cattle upon reaching the alkaline waters around Salt Lake. Despite her best efforts, the thirsty animals couldn't be stopped from drinking the deadly water. Once the tired and weary wagon train, along with the remaining livestock, made it to the Humboldt River, they were attacked by a band of Shoshone Indians. Charley managed to shoot one and stab another before being severely wounded in the arm.

With her arm in a sling, Charley led her battered wagon train to California. On October 29, 1855, the party reached Sacramento Valley, and those who had come west in search of gold purchased provisions to start mining. Charley was among the new prospectors to the area. "We invested in the essentials," Charley recalled in her journal. "Flour was fifty cents a pound, beef twenty-five cents, bacon fifty cents, pickles twenty-five cents, each and everything in proportion. Board, the poorest and the cheapest, was three dollars a day." Charley worked a small claim near the Feather River. Her first attempt to find gold was a disappointment. According to her journal entry, an onslaught of rain made the work nearly impossible. "I did not find my strength sufficient for the business."

Charley eventually abandoned her quest for gold in the California foothills and traveled to Sacramento. There she sought other business opportunities: owning and operating a saloon, running a pack mule service, and buying into a cattle ranch. The cattle ranch was the most successful venture, turning a $30,000 profit in a short time.

In the spring of 1859, Charley relocated to Colorado and began panning for gold around Pikes Peak. After three months wading through the icy waters of the South Platte, she collected two handfuls of nuggets. The outcome was substantially less than she had anticipated and again she left the gold field. She used her findings to open a bakery and a saloon. She made money rapidly, but a bout of mountain fever forced her to give up the business and move to Denver. While she was there she became preoccupied with the news of civil war breaking out. She felt compelled to join the fight against slavery and was sure her disguise would afford her the opportunity to do so.

In September 1862 she enlisted and served with both the Second Colorado Cavalry and the First Colorado Battery. She was assigned to Gen. Samuel R. Curtis's regiment at Keokuk, Iowa, and because of her good penmanship she was detailed to headquarters as a clerk. When the battle of Westport in Missouri broke out, Charley acted as a courier, carrying orders and messages all over the command area. Often she had to travel to the front. Her commanders praised her for her "coolness and bravery."

The first day of the conflict left the Union Army with a number of casualties. General Curtis shared with Charley his desire to ascertain the enemy's battle plans for advancement. Upon hearing this, Charley conceived a way to get into the Rebels' camp and find out their next move. She borrowed a dress, sunbonnet, and other female fixings from one of the laundry women and transformed herself back into the lady she once was. Armed with a basket of eggs, she snuck across enemy lines and into the Southerners' camp.

Her modest, unassuming Missouri country girl act worked well. She was able to gain access to Confederate General Shelby's staff and found out that the Rebels had a fix on the Union Army's cannon company. While eavesdropping on several other conversations around the campsite, Charley learned everything the Rebels knew about the

Yankees' positions. Just as she was about to be escorted out of the area, a courier rode up fast and presented a dispatch to the general. Shelby read the message then jumped to his feet and began barking orders to the troops around him. "Boys," he recalls in his memoir, "I want the pickets along the river doubled! Be quick and quiet! I want twenty of our best men in their saddles quick as lightning."

The soldiers around the camp leapt into action. There was so much activity that no one took notice of Charley as she snuck off into the woods. She watched the disposition of the troops from behind a tree. As the general mounted his horse, he dropped the dispatch on the ground. Charley waited for the camp to clear and then grabbed the message and disappeared into the timber.

Charley made her way down the river, through the dense forest, and back to her regiment without notice. She presented General Curtis with the dispatch and he immediately moved his men into position. The message revealed a surprise attack the Rebel Army was planning to make on Curtis' company. Curtis had enough time to realign his troops just before they were fired upon. Charley was recognized for "bravery displayed in the execution of his perilous trust." She accepted the praise modestly, and with many expressions of thanks to the general for his confidence in her "patriotism and worth to the service." The fighting along the Missouri River was far from over, however.

The Battle of Westport resulted in heavy losses for both sides. Charley was among the injured; Confederate soldiers found her on the ground alongside her dead horse. She had a gunshot wound in her leg and a saber cut in her shoulder. She was taken prisoner by the Rebels and removed to a nearby hospital.

Army doctor Jesse Terry removed the coat from Charley's unconscious form. While inspecting the cut on her shoulder he made the startling discovery that Charley was a woman. He decided to keep the news to himself. He dressed her wound and replaced her jacket, never saying a word to anyone. When Charley regained consciousness she anxiously sought out the doctor who had nursed her back to health.

Terry could tell she was concerned about what he discovered about her and he quickly put her mind at ease. "Your secret is safe with me until you are able to tell me your story," he told her. "There is not time now and this is no place to hear it."

During an exchange of wounded prisoners Charley was freed and transported back to her regiment. While she was recuperating she learned that General Curtis had recommended her for a promotion. She was soon upgraded to First Lieutenant and served out the rest of the war with her unit. Doctor Terry kept his word and never told anyone of Charley's true identity. Charley continued with her life dressed in male attire, and she never failed to provide for her children.

She also never fully abandoned her search for Jamieson. It was while she was on an excursion three miles from Denver City that she came in contact with him again. Charley and Jamieson rode towards one another on a narrow road through a mountain pass. He was riding a mule and from a distance Charley thought there was something familiar about his countenance. As they neared each other she began to realize that it was Jamieson. At roughly the same time he recognized her too. He went for his revolver, but Charley was a second too quick for him.

Charley sent a bullet Jamieson's way and he tumbled off his mule. A bullet from his gun whistled past Charley's head, just missing her. She leveled her revolver at him as he tried to pull himself to his feet. Two more rounds sailed into his body, and he fell down again. He wasn't dead, but Charley was determined to change that.

Just as she removed a second revolver from her holster, two hunters came upon the dispute. The hunters stopped the gunplay, constructed crude irons, and hauled Jamieson off to Denver. Charley followed along behind them, cursing the murderer of her husband the whole way.

Jamieson was taken to a boardinghouse and examined by a physician. Three bullets were removed from his body, but none of the wounds were proved fatal. Within a few weeks he was back on his feet and telling anyone who would listen the whole story of Charley's past life. He told the story of why she was after him and absolved her of blame. He left town and headed for New Orleans.

When word of Charley's true identity made the papers, she became famous. Her efforts during the Civil War were now made all the more astounding in light of the truth of her sex. Charley sought refuge from her newfound popularity in the mountains around Denver. There she married a bartender by the name of H. L. Guerin. The two ran a saloon and a boardinghouse before selling both businesses and mining for gold. The couple had two children together. Charley penned her autobiography in 1861, and subsequent details about her life were published in the *Colorado Transcript* newspaper twenty-four years later by a reporter who claimed to have known Charley and served with her in the cavalry.

Some historians believe there were more than one "Charley Hatfield" and that the story of their lives has intertwined over the years to become one. Still others insist that there was only one person by that name—a daring woman unafraid to venture into areas women seldom entered. Historical records show that she eventually moved to St. Joseph, Missouri and lived out her days surrounded by her loving family.

ETHEL BERRY:
MINER BRIDE OF THE KLONDIKE

"They hit it big up on Rabbit Creek. I'll take the rowboat up to stake us a couple of claims. You put together what we need for the winter."

—Miner Clarence Berry's instructions to

his wife and fellow prospector, Ethel, 1896

Bitterly cold snow flurries pelted the determined features of twenty-one-year-old Ethel Berry's face as she drove her dog sled over the Chilkoot Pass in Alaska. Clad in a pair of men's mackinaw breeches and moccasins, she cracked her whip over the team of animals hauling an enormous mound of supplies behind them. Ethel was slowly making her way to the spot where her husband Clarence was prospecting along the Bonanza Creek, later renamed Rabbit Creek, near the town of Forty Mile. Five months prior to embarking on the arduous journey she had married her childhood sweetheart, promising to follow after him all the days of her life. The newlyweds agreed to spend their honeymoon searching for gold in the Yukon Territory.

In spite of the newspaper articles in the *Seattle Post-Intelligencer* in the late 1890s, which firmly reported that Alaska's frigid terrain was "no place for women," Ethel believed she was strong enough to

Courtesy of Glenbow Archives NA-4319-6.

Ethel Berry and her husband Clarence, posed for a picture with Clarence's brother, Henry and his wife in 1902. The determined female proprietor of a rich Klondike mine stands next to her spouse and is the second from the left.

withstand the brutal trip. The outing to the area where Clarence was panning was a nine-week venture from its starting point in Skagway.

In 1896, the quickest way to reach the remote Bonanza Creek from Skagway was to trek the Inside Passage of Alaska, over a rugged channel that led to British Columbia and Lake Bennett, then travel by boat downstream along the Yukon River, some five hundred miles. Next would be a hike to the town of Dawson and hiring a dog sled team to go to the panning site.

For more than two months, Ethel slept on the ground in a wolf fur-lined sleeping bag and dined primarily on sandwiches made of sticky flapjacks and cold bacon. When she arrived at the camp, Clarence escorted his bride to their primitive new home and left her there to unpack while he worked out on the creeks. The crude structure had no door, windows, or floors, and it wasn't until a hole was cut in the front wall frame that she could even go inside.

As Ethel surveyed the shelter, she remembered a warning she'd received from an elderly prospector she met in Portland, Oregon: "Gold seekers in the heart of Alaska must put up with living in drafty cabins, tents, or caves. Their chief food in winter is bear-fat, and a bath or change of clothing is death." The words echoed inside her head and for a single moment she contemplated returning to her parents' home in central California.

Love for her husband and a severe case of gold fever prompted her to stay and make the best of the difficult living conditions. In an interview several years later, Ethel described the initial hardship she and Clarence faced while setting up house.

We had all the camp-made furniture we needed, a bed and stove—a long, little sheet-iron affair, with two holes on top and a drum to bake in. The fire would burn up and go out if you turned your back on it for a minute. The water we used was all snow or ice, and had to be thawed. If anyone wanted a drink, a chunk of ice had to be thawed and (the hot water) cooled again.

Ethel Bush Berry was born in 1873 in Selma, California, where the average low temperature in the winter was thirty-nine degrees. Her parents were farmers, and although she was raised to endure hard labor and long hours of work, nothing could prepare her for the frozen north.

Clarence spent days away from Ethel searching for a profitable claim. The hope that he could locate a rich stake and provide his wife with the luxury he felt she deserved kept him going back to the frigid

COURTESY OF GLENBOW ARCHIVES NA-1786-8

Ethel Berry sifts through the gravel her husband shovels into her pan near their mine in the Yukon Territory.

creek beds and icy mines. Ethel occupied her time tending to their home. She cleaned and cooked and made flour sack curtains for the windows. The sacks were eventually taken down and cut into strips to use to sift pay dirt in order to find chunks of gold. Ethel took her daily baths by lamplight in a washtub used for collecting pay dirt.

Clarence's early but determined attempts to find gold were unsuccessful. While waiting for the big strike he worked tending bar in Bill McPhee's saloon in Forty Mile to provide an income for his wife and himself. The longest stretch of time Ethel was left alone to fend for herself was five weeks. She knew the separation from her husband was necessary, however. Someone had to stay on their land to keep claim jumpers from overtaking their property.

The time apart from Clarence seemed like an eternity. "I missed him terribly and there was absolutely nothing to do," she later wrote in her memoirs. "No one who has not had a like experience could appreciate even half the misery contained in those words—nothing to do. Just imagine sitting for hours in one's home doing nothing, looking out a scrap of a window and seeing nothing, searching for work and finding nothing. At times when I felt I could not bear another minute of the utter blackness of such an existence, I would walk to a little cemetery nearby for consolation."

With the arrival of spring, Ethel found plenty to occupy her time. When the ice melted and the rocky mountains began to crumble away from the shifting snowpacks, she had new places to pan for gold. While examining chunks of bedrock one day, Ethel unearthed a handful of nuggets from their claim. Not long after her find, Clarence returned with rumors about a major discovery a few miles from their present location. The pair quickly packed their belongings and headed for the spot at Eldorado Creek. Clarence reasoned it was better to have two claims making money than one. Given Ethel's talent for prospecting, she could see to the Bonanza Creek claim and he would work the one at Eldorado Creek, provided they found gold.

The first pan Ethel dipped into the clear, cold water produced favorable results. Layers of gold rock reached from the point where Ethel was panning in the creek to a nearby craggy ledge. The Berrys had hit the mother lode. They sank a shaft deep into the ground and began stockpiling gold-bearing gravel. A stampede to the Klondike followed the news of their discovery and of a few other miners working the creek bed downstream from them. Almost overnight Ethel went from living in solitude to regularly entertaining numerous miners for dinner. The Berry home was always filled with cold, tired, hungry prospectors who enjoyed Ethel's cooking and her company.

In July 1897, a jubilant but exhausted Ethel boarded a steamer bound for Washington. Clarence had decided to remain behind to secure the claim and complete the digging. Ethel was sent ahead with $100,000 in gold dust and nuggets tucked inside a moose-hide bedroll. After she deposited their find in a bank she was going to California to visit her family.

When the ship docked in Seattle she was bombarded by reporters who had heard about the Alaska gold rush and were anxious to interview the brave men and women who were the first to prospect in the frozen territory. Adorned in weathered garments that were kept in place with one of Clarence's belts, and wearing shoes with holes in them, Ethel was the only woman miner among the plethora of men. Journalists called her "The Bride of the Klondike" and her candor in answering the questions posed to her made headlines. A feature article about her exploits circulated around the world and included the advice she would give to women who were thinking about going north.

"Why, to stay away," she said with a slight chuckle. "It's no place for a woman. I mean for a woman alone—one who goes to make a living or a fortune. Yes, there are women going into the mines alone. There were when we came out; widows and lone women to do whatever they could for miners, with the hope of getting big pay.

"It's much better for a man, though, if he has a wife along. The men are not much at cooking up there, and that is the reason they suffer with stomach troubles and some say they did, with scurvy. After a man has worked all day in the diggings he doesn't feel much like cooking. . ."

Although Ethel spoke a great deal about the hardship of living in the glacier wilderness, some newspaper reporters chose to focus more on the riches to be had in Alaska than the difficulties of getting to the fortune. The bold type across the *California Alta News* July 17, 1897, edition read, "Woman Keeps House, Picks Up $10,000 in Nuggets in Spare Time." The headline overshadowed Ethel's comments about the hazards of traveling across the region on a dog sled. "I put on my Alaskan uniform first . . . the heavy flannels, warm dress with short skirt, moccasins, fur coat, cap and gloves, kept my shawl handy to roll up in case of storms, and was rolled in a full robe and bound to the sled, so when it rolled over I rolled with it and many tumbles in the snow I got that way."

Ethel and Clarence's Klondike claim was one of the richest ever found in Alaska. More than $140,000 was pulled out of the mine in a single day. The couple wisely invested their discovery, developing claims throughout the Yukon, further adding to their wealth. The couple used their money to purchase a sprawling farm near her parents' home in Selma. Reporters interested in learning how Clarence and his wife managed to survive the Arctic frontier and return with such a large treasure were surprised by his answer: "I question seriously whether I would have done so well if it had not been for the excellent advice and aid of my wife. I want to give her all the credit that is due to her, and I can assure you that it is a great deal."

In spite of her initial hesitation to go back to the mines at Eldorado and Bonanza Creek, Ethel did return in the spring of 1898. Her sister accompanied her on the second journey over the treacherous Chilkoot Pass. In addition to cooking and caring for her husband and the other prospectors in the area, Ethel carried out various mining duties. She oversaw the diggings at two of the major claims the Berrys owned.

In 1907, the enterprising Berrys began a successful, large-scale dredging operation in the Circle Mining district in the north central region of Alaska. The operation was an excavation activity carried out at least partially underwater. Dredging scraped the gold sediment off the seabed and further increased Clarence and Ethel's strike.

In 1909, Ethel loaned $70,000 in gold nuggets she had found for a display in the Alaskan Yukon Pacific Exposition held in Seattle. After the exposition, Clarence collected the nuggets and sent them on to Tiffany & Co., where the gold was melted down and transformed into a dresser set for his wife.

For more than thirty years, Ethel and Clarence traveled back and forth between their farm in California and their home in Alaska. Clarence passed away during one of those trips in 1930. Ethel then moved to Beverly Hills and died at her home there in 1948 at the age of seventy-five.

FRANCES ALLEN NOYES: MINER ON CANDLE CREEK

"If I can't be in the hills, I would sooner be dead."

—Frances Noyes, 1928

A cluster of tents dotted a strip of frozen earth at the base of a massive glacier in Skagway, Alaska. Beyond the solid layer of ice was a thick forest that followed the contours of a mountain. The numerous trees that covered the ridge were like deep-pile carpet and the grassy scruff under the timbers were red and yellow with the coming of autumn. A clear, cold stream flowed swiftly from the white peaks, spilling over the layers of compacted snow. Pieces of the iceberg broke off and fell into the freezing water.

Frances Noyes, a pretty, determined woman dressed in a heavy wool coat, thick-soled, knee-high boots, and wool gloves traveled along a gravel trail running parallel to the stream.

Frances stopped momentarily to plunge a gold mining pan into the rocky creek bed and sift through the pebbles. Like hundreds of other miners that rushed to Alaska in 1898 looking for gold, Frances was confident she would discover a fortune. The biting wind and snow flurries that cut across her path did not deter her from her work. She glanced around at the setting and smiled.

Frances Noyes and her husband Thomas outside their tent near Otter Creek, Alaska.

She was invigorated by her surroundings. "If there ever was a woman prospector, it was Frances," Frances's nephew William Simonds recalled of his aunt. "She was never as content in her life as she was mining in the Alaskan wilderness."

Frances and her husband, Thomas C. Noyes, searched for gold along Otter Creek near Skagway from September 1899 to February 1900. She was one of a handful of women miners who dared to brave the sub-zero temperatures of the isolated Klondike. The intrepid female pioneer actually chose mining as her second career. Her first job was as a stage actress. Beautiful and talented, she spent years entertaining audiences in boomtowns across the Old West. One audience member was Thomas Noyes, a man she fell in love with and wanted to marry in spite of his family's objections and without whom, she may not have ever realized her true calling.

"I shall conduct no training school for actresses," Montana mining tycoon John Noyes declared. He sent his son Tom a withering glare. The boy had obviously been taken in by a pretty face, but this was not the type of woman he had in mind as a wife for his son. She'd been married and divorced, and that scandal had hardly quieted when a new one had erupted.

The full weight of his father's displeasure only strengthened Tom's resolve. "You have $2,500 in a trust fund that you are holding for me, have you not, Father?"

"Yes."

"Well, give me that. I will start out for myself, and you can cut me off without a cent."

Tom had loved Frances Allen ever since he first saw her in a theatrical production. His father thought Tom was too young to marry and Frances too infamous to be his bride, but Tom intended to marry her, and soon, for Frances had another would-be suitor from New Orleans who was stalking her from state to state and might soon appear in Butte.

Tom did not change his mind, though his father continually dredged up the infamy of Frances's past, starting with her divorce from Samuel Allen earlier in 1897. The newspapers had reported every titillating development. According to one account, Samuel Allen had told his friends that his ex-wife "is a good woman, but has a passion for money, a siren who uses her charms to infatuate men to the point where they lavish their wealth upon her, but she never strays from the straight and narrow path."

A report in Spokane's *Spokesman* entitled "She's An Actress, Ex-Prosecuting Attorney Objects to the Life" claimed, "The wreck of this family commenced about the time of the society circus at Natatorium Park in 1895, when Mrs. Allen rode two horses bareback. Mr. Allen did not enjoy this exhibition, and the family was never a happy one."

Tom suspected his father had seen that article. He was certain the electrifying accounts had convinced his father to forbid him to marry the woman he loved. The newspapers, in Tom's opinion, wrongly made Frances sound like a beautiful but heartless, money-hungry tease. Tom's father certainly believed this and reminded his son that no respectable woman would flaunt herself on stage unless she was out to snare a rich husband. But Tom knew Frances did not care about money. She would marry him with his small trust fund and no prospects of inheriting his father's huge fortune. She would marry him for him.

What worried Tom was the threat hanging over Frances's life. A would-be suitor, Alfred Hildreth, was stalking Frances, and his actions had steadily become more dangerous. At the Leland Hotel in Chicago, Hildreth had lain in wait for his mistress for five days. The Southerner confronted Frances in the lobby, and witnesses said Frances agreed to dine with him at a downtown restaurant, where the man brandished a carving knife while declaring he would do something desperate if she wouldn't have him. He had followed Frances through several states, and his ardor increased every time he caught up with her. Tom knew Alfred could show up at any time.

Newspapers in Chicago and New York recorded the tales of Hildreth's obsession. The *Chicago Chronicle* carried one story that made Tom's blood boil:

Alfred J. Hildreth loves Mrs. Frances Allen with such true and ardent affection that he has followed her 5,000 miles to prove it. Even though Mr. Allen secured a divorce from his wife because she rode bareback at a charity circus in Spokane, Wash., attired in the reddest of red silken tights, Hildreth says she is dear to him. Mrs. Allen, however, does not return the feeling of young Hildreth, and she has spent many weary hours moving from one city to another to escape the devoted lover.

The tights had been pink, but Tom didn't bother to correct the story. Frances Allen belonged to him, and neither Alfred Hildreth nor Tom's own father was going to stand in the way of a wedding.

And Arabella Frances Patchen Allen did not care that Tom's father disapproved of her life on the stage. She intended to marry his son.

Of all the men who had pursued her since she had left Spokane after the fateful circus ride, Tommy was the one she truly loved. Her first marriage had been troubled from the start. On the day of her wedding to Samuel Allen in 1892, when she was barely eighteen, the groom had disappeared. His drunken companions had held a "special session" and voted to continue the wedding anyway, with a different groom. After several good-natured votes were taken among the unmarried men, each of whom had voted for himself, Samuel had finally reappeared, and the vows were spoken.

For a few years she had enjoyed the social life that was part of being married to a prominent lawyer. Samuel had even given his consent for her participation in the charity circus at Natatorium Park, since half the money would go to the family of a boy who had broken his back in a barrel slide. Her husband had stalked out in a rage when he discovered his beautiful young wife in form-fitting tights and short blue skirt, riveting the attention of every person in the place.

Samuel's outrage had resulted in a huge quarrel, and she'd left his fine home for good that August. By April of the following year, she had succeeded on the stage. She knew if she hadn't ridden in the society circus, she might still be married to Samuel and living well, but by leaving Spokane and taking parts in productions in Bradford, Pennsylvania, she'd achieved some success of her own. And her acting career had allowed her to meet Tom Noyes.

The 1897 wedding of Tom Noyes and Frances Allen did not compare in any way to Tom's sister, Ruth Noyes's wedding to Arthur Heinz, which linked two prosperous mining families and was celebrated as the most brilliant wedding ever held in Montana. Tom and Frances were married in a small, quiet ceremony and started mining together in Skagway, Alaska, at the foot of a glacier on Otter Creek.

Tom knew he was a lucky man. Not many women would have smiled through the bitter cold and long darkness of an Alaskan winter. Unlike the California gold rush, few women had hurried to the rush in the frozen northland. But his petite, vivacious Frances was one of a handful of women truly interested in mining. She loved the open country and the freedom from the society that had scorned her.

Frances was as eager as Tom to move on when Otter Creek didn't provide the wealth they were seeking. They headed for wide-open, lawless Nome, located at the edge of the Seward Peninsula on the Bering Sea.

Gold had been discovered at Anvil Creek, and by the spring of 1900, somewhere between twenty and thirty thousand "stampeders" had come to Nome.

Camped above the tide line with thousands of others, Frances, who stood approximately two inches shorter than five feet tall, helped shovel sand into the portable rockers used to sift out the fine gold. Many people believed that the ocean was depositing gold at high tide. Tents and rockers stretched for miles along the beach.

Tom was appointed to a four-year term as a U.S. Commissioner for the Fairhaven District of Alaska, and soon Frances and Tom were again moving in the upper circles of society, albeit a much more flamboyant elite than the stuffy and conventional social strata they'd left behind. Tom's knowledge of mining and his impeccable character, dubbed "pure gold" by one of the men he worked with on several claims, earned report in lawless Nome.

Tom wanted to find the Alaska mother lode, and Frances always followed where he led. He learned from one of the native people in the area that gold was easier to get on Candle Creek. Frances put away her silks and lace and followed Tom hundreds of miles north to Candle Creek, where they staked several claims.

Frances experienced "mushing" by dogsled and began to learn more and more about prospecting. Alaskan newspapers covered some of the adventures of the prospecting newlyweds, reporting that they endured "perilous trips, lost trails, [and] climbs over glacier fields, where steps had to be cut with an ax." More than once Frances was credited with saving her husband's life. After a time, their claims paid off, and Tom became known as "King of the Candle." He built a home for himself and Frances, where anyone was welcome.

In 1902 Tom's father died, and Tom inherited an interest in a hotel in Seattle. Success piled on success, and Frances and Tom began to alternate between harsh conditions and adventures in Alaska with society teas and balls in Seattle and Butte.

In 1905, Tom and Frances adopted a half-Eskimo girl, Bonnie, who was approximately five years old. During the winter she attended school in Butte; in the summer she often returned to Alaska with her parents.

As their success in Candle grew, Tom conceived of a plan to bring water to the rich placer diggings. In the autumn of 1907, he left for New York to obtain $200,000 to finance the completion of the Bear Creek ditch. Frances stayed at Candle to manage their interests.

He'd barely arrived in New York when a financial panic hit, jeopardizing the nation's economy. As a result, no bank would loan him money for a project in Alaska, and funds were so tight Tom had to pawn his watch and jewelry to pay his hotel bills. The bank in Candle and the bank in Nome were threatened with a run by frightened customers eager to get their money into their own hands.

In an unprecedented feat of courage and strength, Frances once again came to her husband's rescue, only this time she saved his financial life. Pawning her jewelry to raise ten thousand dollars, Frances mushed across the frozen Artic tundra in the dead of winter to deliver the proceeds. The story was printed in the *Seattle Times* and many other newspapers.

With only a driver for her team of malamutes, she started out across the hundreds of miles of ice and snow, the thermometer so low it almost faded from view. Through the short days and into the nights this brave woman trudged on through the snow. Many days were needed for the journey, but the news that the money was coming had spread a better feeling in Nome and the bank was able to weather the storm until relief should arrive. The journey made by Mrs. Noyes was one of the most heroic ever attempted by a woman on her own initiative in the far North, and when she reached Nome she was accorded a welcome that was commensurate with her feat.

The bank was saved, and a woman had been the agent.

Unfortunately, two years later Tom's bank failed, and his claims at Candle were lost. Tom had made a critical mistake—failing to use his official bank title when he signed checks—that left him personally liable when the bank failed. Tom and Frances retreated to Tongass Island near Ketchikan. In 1913 Tom ventured out to try his luck during a stampede to the Shushana gold strike. Shortly afterward, Frances joined him. There the harsh conditions of the Alaskan goldfields took their final toll.

Although they met with some success, one of the prospecting trips they took resulted in disaster. Days on the trail in temperatures as low as fifty degrees below zero with little shelter and poor food left Tom a "physical wreck."

On December 15, 1915, Tom was hospitalized in Port Simpson General Hospital in British Columbia. Frances slept on a cot in his room, watching over and caring for him. Later, with Frances and his mother at his side, he was taken to a hospital in St. Louis, but he died of pneumonia on February 2, 1916.

Stunned and heartbroken, their fortune gone, Frances returned alone to Tongass Island. She received a letter that spring from one of their former partners recalling Tom and Frances's early days at Otter Creek.

Nearly 17 years ago you said goodbye to me on the platform at Seattle and you knew that you were saying farewell to a friend who would have done anything for you. I have not altered.

I am just the same William you knew at Otter Creek and in our little camp at the foot of the glacier.

The letter goes on to remember Tom.

I shall never realize that Tommy is dead. Since I left you I have been in many places and had dealings with many men, but I have never come across another Tommy, he was just pure gold. I was trying to think last night if I could remember him being out of temper or cross, but I could not, and we had some trying times. It is a great thing to have had a partner in life who you can look forward to meeting, to whom you can hold your hand out to and look straight in the eye and say "Tommy, I am glad to see you."

Perhaps there may be another Klondike for us beyond the clouds; if there is I could ask for nothing better than my two dear friends of the glacier should be my partners again.

The writer advised Frances not to return to Alaska, but the woman who had married at eighteen, divorced at twenty-three, and married again that same year to a man she cherished despite the scorn and anger of her father-in-law, returned to the northern land she loved.

She kept body and soul together by managing the Nakat Inlet cannery store, but her love of the Alaskan wilderness eventually lured her away from civilization. She went back to prospecting, where everything she'd learned from her beloved Tommy allowed her to prosper.

Frances married again at the age of forty-five to William Muncaster, who was fifteen years younger. Despite the age difference, Bill had been smitten for years with Frances. He'd sent her love letters and stopped in to visit her between trips to survey Alaska for the Coast and Geodetic Survey. Her daughter Bonnie accompanied Frances and her new stepfather on their honeymoon trip to Alaska's goldfields.

Frances and William lived in a cabin on Wellesley Lake. They prospected and often went on fishing and hunting trips even when the temperature dipped to fifty below zero. Tom's memory, however, never faded from Frances's mind. Visiting a place she and Tom had stayed during the Shushana gold strike, she wrote in her diary, "Everything looks different. Everything is different."

One thing that never changed was Frances's love of prospecting. She and William visited their claims until 1946, at which time Frances was seventy-two years old and living in Haines, a small town in southeastern Alaska.

The woman who scandalized Spokane with her daring ride in pink tights, the actress who caused a mining tycoon to shun his heir, the woman who saved her husband's bank with a grueling trek across the frozen northland, the unlikely prospector who loved Alaska so much she spent fifty-four years there, died on October 28, 1952. William Muncaster provided the press with clippings and stories about her life in Alaska, including a final letter he wrote for the local newspaper.

Dear Sir,

Please publish this letter, for I wish to thank with all my heart all the people, young and old alike, in the town of Haines, Alaska, and the adjoining vicinities North, South, East and West for the unbelievable 100 percent respect shown by them at Mrs. Frances Muncaster's final rites. I thank you.

William Muncaster

FERMINIA SARRAS:
NEVADA'S COPPER MINING QUEEN

"We do not see any reason why women should not engage in mining as well as men. If they can rock a cradle, they can run a car; if they can wash and scrub, they can pick and shovel."

Editorial comments by the staff at Virginia City,
Nevada's newspaper *The Territorial Enterprise*, 1871

A strong, but dainty hand dipped a pen into an inkwell and scratched a name in a ledger at the Esmeralda County courthouse in 1881. Written in big, bold letters was the name "Ferminia Sarras. Spanish Lady, Belleville." Every miner in the area was required to register in the tax record and this feisty, forty-one-year-old prospector, often mistaken for being an Indian or Mexican, wanted to list her true heritage. The form completed, Ferminia proudly exited the building and marched off to her mining claims in the western Nevada hills.

A hard rock miner who made and lost a fortune in numerous silver and copper diggings, she was considered by her peers to be a formidable force. Ferminia had a talent for locating valuable ore and was tough enough to defend her mine. The diminutive, slightly overweight woman carried a six-shooter in the folds of her dress to ward off anyone who considered jumping her claim.

Ferminia was born in July 1840 in Nicaragua, a descendant of the noble Contreras family who governed the entire region in the 16th century. Several years before leaving Nicaragua, Ferminia married Pablo Flores and the couple had four little girls. In 1876, the ambitious thirty-six-year-old woman traveled to San Francisco in search of a better life and the immense opportunity for wealth in the nearby goldfields. Whether or not Pablo accompanied his family on the journey is unknown—some historical records indicate that Pablo made his way to the mining district of Nevada without family. After arriving in San Francisco, Ferminia traveled through California and on into Nevada in 1880 with only her daughters by her side.

The prospective miner initially settled in Virginia City, Nevada, after she learned of the discovery of silver in the outlying hills. Looking out of place in a black taffeta dress and wearing a gold cross pendant, Ferminia invested the little funds she had in mining equipment and supplies. She decided to leave her two youngest girls at the Nevada Orphans Asylum before setting out to stake a claim with her two oldest children.

Loaded down with picks, pans, axes, food, and clothing, the three hiked more than one hundred miles from Virginia City to the mining camp of Belleville and then proceeded on to Candelaria. A census from 1875 shows that Pablo was in the vicinity at the same time, but there is no record that the two searched for silver together. And while Ferminia filed her first claim in April of 1883, her husband's name is not associated with the find. Some speculate that he had died by that time.

The weather in the high desert where Ferminia looked for silver, copper, and gold was extreme. During the winter months, temperatures plunged below freezing and in the summer, the sun's hot rays were relentless. The weather, though, would not overwhelm the lady miner: She would trek for days at a time carrying a forty-pound pack on her back. The possibility of a great fortune spurred her on, and after scouring the countryside for more than two years, Ferminia finally located valuable silver ore on a site she named "The Central American."

When Ferminia wasn't prospecting, she was spending the fruits of her labor in the mining camps that dotted the Candelaria Hills. She splurged on the finest food and champagne and kept company with a variety of miners, most of whom were considerably younger than she.

She was also drawn to gunslingers, since they would be valuable in defending her claims. One such suitor lost his life defending her property from thieves. In early 1881, another of the men she became involved with left her with a new baby to care for and disappeared. On January 25, 1881, she gave birth to her fifth child, a son named Joseph A. Marshall. She carried the newborn from one boom camp to another, never deviating from her mission to stake more claims.

In 1885, Ferminia moved her family into a small house in the railroad town of Luning, Nevada, near Tonopah. After locating a series of copper mines in the area, she purchased a ranch in Sand Springs, a spot east of Fallon, and a toll road in Death Valley. The toll road proved to be one of the most profitable ventures she ever entered into. During the years when her mines were not producing, she lived off the funds earned from the road. In addition to supporting her family on the income, she helped destitute miners passing through the area who needed a meal and a place to sleep.

Determined that she would one day find a strike that would yield millions, Ferminia moved south to Silver Peak, a location

Photograph of the town named for Ferminia Sarras. This is the business district of Main Street in 1907.

rumored to be rich with silver and copper. She registered numerous claims in the area, none of which panned out to be worth much at all.

It wasn't until 1900 that she managed to make the significant money she dreamed she could from her various mines. Lucrative ore deposits found near Tonopah prompted investors to scramble to buy up claims. Ferminia's holdings in the vicinity included abundant copper diggings and she sold off twenty-five claims at $8,000 a piece. She celebrated her windfall in San Francisco in the way she always did whenever she got a little ahead financially: staying in fancy hotels, buying elegant clothing, and dining at the most expensive eateries.

As a result of the copper discovery, the area around Tonopah grew at an alarming rate. By 1905, the region was in desperate need of a railroad depot to accommodate the miners and businessmen who were traveling back and forth between Tonopah and the nearby camp of Goldfield. Railroad executives decided against paying the landowners in the area the outrageous price they were asking for their property to build the depot. They chose instead to create a new town north of the Caldelaria Hills and build the depot there. Ferminia's reputation as Nevada territory's "Copper Queen" prompted railroad executives to name the spot Mina.

Mina was a prosperous location and Ferminia benefited greatly from the influx of people to the town.

Over the years, she amassed a handsome sum selling off her land to the brokerage firms and entrepreneurs. Although she had relinquished many of her holdings in the district, she still possessed many profitable mines throughout the state.

By 1907, residents from Tonopah to Reno estimated that she was worth more than a quarter of a million dollars. With the exception of $10,000, which was deposited in a Los Angeles bank, Ferminia kept the majority of her wealth hidden at her homestead. She believed banks were more likely to be robbed than she would be. Indeed, the only money that was ever taken from her was the funds in the bank, although not exactly in the way she had feared. Doming Velasco, one of Ferminia's lovers, managed to withdraw the money before leaving the country for South America.

In her mid-seventies, Ferminia decided to return to Luning and retire from prospecting. Her son Joseph took over the everyday duties of the mining operations she still possessed and continued to include his mother in any discussions about their disposition. He recognized that her considerable knowledge of the business was the key to her success, and ultimately his. In her final days, Ferminia was surrounded by her children, sons and daughters-in-law, and numerous grandchildren, many of whom she had named claims after.

Before passing away on February 1, 1915, Ferminia made out a will so that several of her loved ones received a portion of her estate. The claims she owned in Giroux Canyon, Nevada, are still being mined today and Ferminia's descendants continue to benefit from her findings there.

Ferminia Sarras died when she was seventy-five years old, and the Spanish Belle was buried at the Luning cemetery and a massive monument was placed over her grave. Vandals demolished the headstone, but nothing could erase Ferminia's place in mining history. The day of her funeral the local newspaper, *The Western Nevada Miner,* proclaimed her to have been "one of the last of those brave spirits who dared the desert's fierce glare in Nevada's primitive days and blazed the trails that others might follow."

GLOSSARY OF MINING TERMS

Assayer: A person who tests mineral ores to see if they contain any valuable metals.

Argonaut: A name given to the thousands of people who flocked to California during the gold rush in 1849.

Backer: A person who provides the money for mining a claim. A miner would do the actual panning and would share the gold with the backer.

Bonanza: A rich body of ore or a rich part of a deposit; a mine is in bonanza when it is operating profitably.

Claim: A piece of land that a miner has made his own. All rights to the minerals in that claim are his. A typical claim was about fifty feet by four hundred feet.

Coyoting: Burrowing narrow holes into the earth in search of gold; the hole that was dug was usually just deep enough for a miner to stand in and shovel dirt out of comfortably. Like a coyote slowly emerging from his den, the only thing that could be seen of a prospector while coyoting was his head.

Cradle: A long wooden trough used by miners to separate gold flakes and nuggets from mud and silt from the bottom of a creek bed. They would fill the trough with mud and water, and then they would rock it until the mud separated from the heavier minerals, like gold.

Forty-niner: Another handle given to the pioneers who went west with the gold rush in 1849.

Float: A general term for loose fragments of ore or rock, especially on a hillside below an outcropping ledge or vein. It was also a reference to the fine gold that floats in panning and other operations and is lost.

Grubstaking: Working a claim using money supplied by a backer. The miner does all the mining work, and the backer provides the money and tools needed to mine in return for a share of the gold that is found.

High-grading: The theft or concealment of valuable ore by miners for personal profit.

Humbug: A name used to describe a claim that had been worked but in which no gold was ever found.

Lead: Commonly used synonym for ledge or lode. Many mining location notices describe the locator's claim as extending a certain number of feet along and so many feet on each side of the lode, lead, vein, or ledge.

Mother lode: A name given for a rich find; a rich ore deposit from which a placer is derived; the mother rock of a placer.

Ore: Any natural combination of minerals. Especially one from which a metal or metals can be profitably extracted. Commonly a mixture of one or more of the following: quartz, gold, copper, silver, sulfur, iron, and nickel.

Pack Train: Pack trains were used to transport the bare necessities to miners. They usually consisted of 5 or more horses or mules and a few men.

Placer: Gold that has been washed away from its mother lode (or source) and deposited in small cracks, holes, or sand bar in the mainstream of a river.

Pocket: A cavity filled with ore, or a rich deposit of precious metal.

Panning: Using a shallow, wide pan to search for gold. Scooping up water and mud from a creek bed, the miner would swish the water to separate the sand and drift from larger rocks that might have been gold.

Rocker: A small digging bucket mounted on two rocker arms in which sand and gravel are agitated by oscillation in water to collect gold.

Salting: A practice used to sell a worthless claim. The seller sprinkled a few flecks of gold around the claim. When the buyer inspected the claim, he saw the planted flecks, and may have thought the claim was valuable.

Sluice box: An elongated wooden or metal trough with riffles, over which gravel is washed to recover gold.

Stake: Another name for a claim; a permanent interest, as in an enterprise or a mine.

Sourdough: An old-fashioned and seasoned prospector; a miner who lived in Alaska more than one season.

Tailings: The valueless minerals and other refuse material resulting from the washing, concentration, or treatment of gold ore.

BIBLIOGRAPHY

GENERAL REFERENCES

Banks, Leo. *Stalwart Women*. Phoenix: Arizona Highways Books, 1999.

Beebee, Lucius, and Charles Clegg. *The American West*. New York: E.P. Dutton & Company, 1955.

Bowman, John S. *The American West Year by Year*. New York: Crescent Books, 1995.

Brown, Dee. *The Gentle Tamers: Women of the Old West*. Lincoln: University of Nebraska Press, 1958.

Calhoon, F. D. *California Gold and the Highgraders*. Sacramento: Cal-Con Press, 1988.

Convis, Charles L. *Miners: True Tales of the Old West*. Carson City, NV: Pioneer Press, 1998.

Dillinger, William C. *The Gold Discovery*. Santa Barbara: California Department of Parks and Recreation, 1990.

Lardner, W.B., and M. J. Brock. *History of Placer and Nevada Counties.* Los Angeles: Historic Record Company, 1924.

Lingerfelter, Richard. *The Hardrock Miners.* Berkeley: University of California Press, 1974.

McLeod, Norman. *Gold, Guns & Gallantry.* Newcastle, CA: Goldridge Press, 1987.

Moynihan, Ruth, Susan Armitage, and Christiane Dischamp, eds. *So Much to Be Done.* Lincoln: University of Nebraska Press, 1990.

Niethammer, Carolyn. *The Lure of Gold: Women Who Made the West.* New York: Avon Books, 1980.

Rawls, James J., and Richard Orsi. *A Golden State: Mining and Economic Development in Gold Rush California.* Berkeley: University of California Press, 1999.

Reiter, Joan S. *The Women.* Alexandria, VA: Time Life Book Series, 1978.

Savage, Jeff. *Gold Miners of the Old West.* Springfield, NJ: Enslow Publishers, Inc., 1995.

Schmitt, Martin, and Dee Brown. *The Settlers' West.* New York: Bonanza Books, 1964.

Sheafer, Silvia Anne. *Frontier Women.* Glendale, CA: Historical California Journal Publications, 1992.

Sherrow, Victoria. *Life During the Gold Rush.* San Diego: Lucent Books, 1998.

Steber, Rick. *Women of the West.* Princeville, OR: Bonanza Publishing, Ltd., 1988.

Wallace, Robert. *The Miners.* Alexandria, VA: Time Life Book Series, 1976.

Ward, Geoffrey. *The West: An Illustrated History.* New York: Little, Brown & Company, 1996.

Wilson, Graham. *The Klondike Gold Rush.* Whitehorse, Yukon: Wolf Creek Books, 1997.

Zanjani, Sally. *A Mine of Her Own.* Lincoln: University of Nebraska Press, 1987.

Zauner, Phyllis. *Those Spirited Women of the Early West.* Sonoma, CA: Zanel Publications, 1994.

BABY DOE TABOR

Bancroft, Caroline. *Silver Queen: The Fabulous Story of Baby Doe Tabor.* Boulder: Johnson Printing Company, 1955.

Burke, John. *The Legend of Baby Doe Tabor.* New York: G. P. Putnam's Sons, 1974.

Life Magazine. Wallace, Robert "Pioneer Women Good and Bad." May 11, 1959: 2–6.

ELLEN NAY

The Fallon Standard. "Ellen Nay Buried in Tonopah." April 9, 1947.

Nevada State Journal. "Leasers Active at Ellendale." August 19, 1909.

———. "Reports Another Ellendale Strike." July 4, 1909.

———. "Rich Ore from Ellendale Mines." July 20, 1909.

Tonopah Sun. "Goldfield News." June 21, 1909.

Tonopah Times-Bonanza. "Ellen Nay Passes." April 4, 1947.

DAME SHIRLEY

Clappe, Louise A.K.S. *The Shirley Letters.* New York: Ballantine Books, 1971.

Old West Magazine. Eller, Virginia "A Lady Goes to the Mines." Fall 1976: 15–22.

Rawls, J. *Dame Shirley & the Gold Rush.* Orlando: Steck-Vaugn, 1992.

BIBLIOGRAPHY

NELLIE CASHMAN

Clum, John P. "Nellie Cashman." *Arizona Historical Review* 3 (1931): 9–34.

Fischer, Ronald. *Nellie Cashman: Frontier Angel.* Honolulu: Talei Publishing, 2000.

Haigh, Jane, and Claire Rudolf Murphy. *Gold Rush Women.* Anchorage: Alaska Northwest Books, 1997.

Hazen-Hammond, Susan. "Nellie Cashman: Tombstone's Angel with a Dirty Face." *Arizona Highway,* February 1987: 13, no. 1

Ledbetter, Suzann. *Nellie Cashman: Prospector and Trailblazer.* El Paso: Texas Western Press, 1993.

GERTRUDE PECKWITH

Lee Adams, Former Sierra County, California Sheriff, conversation with the author, April 20, 2007.

Mountain Messenger. Downieville, CA. "Peckwith Funeral Pending," August 28, 1958.

Sinnott, James L. *History of Sierra County.* Volcano, CA: California Traveler Books, 1975.

FRANCES WILLIAMS

Apple Tree Historical Record. "First Woman in Goldfield Carson City, Nevada." November 13, 1977.

The Nevada Observer. "History of Esmeralda County, Nevada." November 4, 2005.

The Pueblo Chieftan. "The Pioneer Woman of Goldfield Tonopah, Nevada." April 23, 1905.

LILLIAN MALCOLM

Goldfield News. "Petticoat Prospectors." October 13, 1905.

Reno Evening Gazette. "Women Miners." June 14, 1910.

Reno Gazette-Journal. "Women of the West" Reno, NV. March 20, 1988.

JOSIE PEARL

Nevada Review-Miner. "Gold in Them Hills." September 19, 1930.

Reno Evening Gazette. "Chasing Rainbows." May 14, 1938.

Schulmerich, Alma. *Josie Pearl.* Salt Lake City: Desert Book Company, 1963.

CHARLEY HATFIELD

Chartier, J., and Chris Enss. *She Wore A Yellow Ribbon*. Guilford, CT: Globe Pequot Press, 2004.

Colorado Transcript. "Golden, Colorado." January–March 1885.

Daily Chronicle. "Leadville, Colorado." July 15, 1879.

Guerin, E. J. *Mountain Charley; or the Adventures of Mrs. E. J. Guerin, Who Was Thirteen in Male Attire*. Norman: University of Oklahoma Press, 1968.

Hall, Richard. *Patriot in Disguise: Women Warriors of the Civil War*. New York: Marlowe & Company, 1993.

Hattaway, Herman. *Historical Times Illustrated Encyclopedia of the Civil War*. New York: Harper & Row, 1986.

Rocky Mountain News. "Denver, Colorado." "The Ballad of Charlie Hatfield" September 10, 1859, (Pg. 23).

ETHEL BERRY

Berry, C. J. "*The Bushes and the Berrys*." Yukon Archives Web site www.tc.gov.yk.ca.

Haigh, Jane, and Claire Rudolf Murphy. *Gold Rush Women*. Anchorage: Alaska Northwest Books, 1997.

San Francisco Examiner. "San Francisco, California." August 1, 1897.

Yukon Archives Web site www.tc.gov.yk.ca

FRANCES ALLEN NOYES

Daily Alaska Empire (Juneau), October 31 and November 4, 1952.

Letters of William Muncaster, Emma C. Patchen, Dr. William W. Graves, and Capt. W.H.K., Alaska Historical Library, Juneau.

Mining and Engineering World, February 1916.

New York Journal, September 1897.

Seattle Sunday Times, June 14, 1908.

Spokane Review, September 22, 1892.

The Spokesman (Spokane, WA), June 15, 1899.

Ward, Louetta. *Inventory of the Frances Noyes Muncaster Papers 1850–1952* Juneau: Alaska Historical Society, 1985.

FERMINIA SARRAS

Cleere, Jan. *More Than Petticoats: Remarkable Nevada Woman.* Guilford, CT: Globe Pequot Press, 2005.

Hulse, James W. *The Silver State: Nevada's Heritage Reinterpreted.* Reno: University of Nevada Press, 1991.

Meadows, Lorena Edwards. *A Sagebrush Heritage: The Story of Ben Edwards and His Family.* San Jose: Harland-Young Press, 1972.

INDEX